SEASIDE *Style*

SEASIDE
Style

Eleanor Lynn Nesmith
photography by Steven Brooke

RIZZOLI
NEW YORK

To my father and my sister
And to Carolyn and Daniel
—E.L.N.

For Suzanne and Miles
—S.B.

First published in the United States of America in 2003 by
RIZZOLI INTERNATIONAL PUBLICATIONS, INC.
300 Park Avenue South, New York, NY 10010
www.rizzoliusa.com

ISBN: 0-8478-2578-7
LCCN: 2003104984

Designed by Judy Geib and Aldo Sampieri

Printed and bound in the U.K.

2004 2005 2006 2007 / 10 9 8 7 6 5 4 3 2

CONTENTS

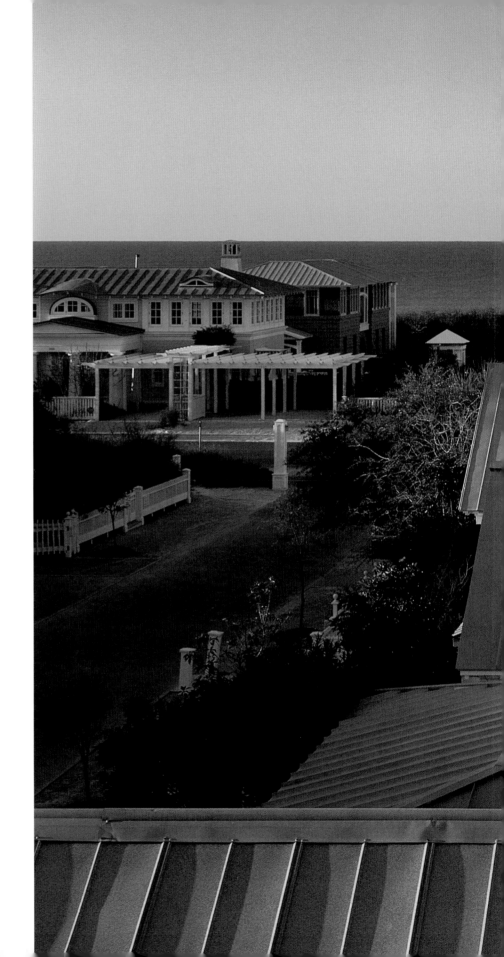

INTRODUCTION

6

A house along the water has an unwavering allure. I spent my childhood holidays in Sunset Beach, North Carolina. Summers were swimming in churning Atlantic waves, picking up shells, building castles in the sand, and chasing sand crabs after sundown. Autumns were oysters roasting on an open grill and fisherman casting nets in the surf for mullet. At the first hint of warm weather, our Boston Whaler was launched for exploring winding estuaries on the rising tide.

From my earliest memories our family beach cottage possessed a unique fascination. It was a place to savor the simple pleasures of summer and a place to simply have fun. A ubiquitous wooden structure set on piers, the house possessed neither architectural ambitions nor fashionable aspirations. Yet, its form did follow function. The elevated stature avoided rising water during hurricanes and captured prevailing winds on a hot summer day.

Overlooking the tidal marsh, the cottage boasted no television, no central heat, and no air conditioning. Instead, operable windows swung open to capture a near-constant breeze off the Atlantic Ocean. Wet swim suits, sandy feet, and relentless humidity came with the territory, so furnishings and fabrics were basically indestructible. Of course, there was an outdoor shower with less than adequate pressure and never enough hot water.

Certain houses, like certain people, possess their own sense of style. Did that simple square box of a cottage have style? Absolutely. But it was not a style that would ever go in or out of fashion—it was and still is an attitude, a state of mind, a way of life.

THE SPIRIT OF THE SETTING

Beloved houses and places have a unique essence and a distinctive aesthetic. With history on their side, these treasured settings around the world garner our affections and engender our collective memories.

The holiday town of Seaside along the Gulf of Mexico in the Florida Panhandle possesses many of the same attributes of historic settlements and cities that one can't help but love. It originates with a desire to embrace the things that make an area special, that make it true—whether a cottage by the sea, a small town, a grand urban park, or a culturally cohesive region.

With a fetching mix of charm and charisma, Seaside strikes a deep chord. It is a place where people still sit on porches, lean on picket fences, gather in the coffee shop, and meet and greet in the street. Days can be wasted sunstruck and silly on the beach. Lunches of freshly caught red fish, vine-ripe tomatoes, and crisp white wine linger into late afternoon celebrations. Modica Market, Bud & Alley's, the post office, and the glorious white sandy beach are all within easy walking distance of home. Strolling, biking, and lounging, as well as diving in the surf and relaxing under an umbrella are perfect ways to bide the time.

The houses of Seaside with their familiar forms respond to the climate, but these iconic images of home also evoke memories of summers long ago and foster uncomplicated activities of the past. Simplicity, optimism, and a sense of easy living rule. Screen porches offer shady and sheltered outdoor living rooms. Picket fences define small yards of native landscapes. Rocking chairs and hammocks encourage relaxation. Thunder cracks at the windows. Rain pounds tin roofs. Breezeways are an invitation to watch lazy clouds drift by or spend a few hours with a book. White curtains billow in a breeze off the gulf. The setting sun bathes widow's walks with a warm glow.

The ability of architecture to amplify the attraction of its settings and define our experiences is often underrated or misunderstood. Free of suburban distractions and glaring noises, the mind can float freely to relish a sunset, to hear the sounds of the waves and the wind, and to see the constellations. Perhaps it is the association of water with leisure, an unhurried pace, or the memories of a carefree time that draws people back to the shore year after year. Or maybe it is a craving to escape the priorities and pressures that dictate daily experience and return to essentials—if only as reassurance of what is essential.

PARTICULARS OF THIS PLACE

The marginal world where the land meets the sea appears infinite. The aquamarine waters, the thick salt air, and cerulean blue skies engage the senses and encourage a sense of well-being. Florida is bordered by more miles of shoreline, estuaries, bays, and beaches than any other state in the country. The southern part of the state is a tropical climate with an array of international influences, while the Panhandle enjoys four distinct seasons and is more socially and culturally aligned with lower Alabama and Georgia than Miami Beach.

A century ago when the Atlantic Coast and South Florida were experiencing a development boom, the Gulf Coast beaches along the Panhandle were less accessible. Expanding railroads, highways, and waterways of the early twentieth century bypassed the northwest corner of the state. By the 1950s and '60s when developers discovered Fort Walton Beach, Destin, and Panama City, their schemes sorely lacked the architectural ambitions of the Flaglers, Merricks, and Ringlings of south and central Florida.

Then in the early 1980s, the tide started to turn, if ever so slowly, in a small corner of northwest Florida along the Gulf of Mexico. With eighty acres and an extraordinary vision, Robert and Daryl Davis set out to build an old-fashioned beach town from scratch. Blessed with lush native landscape and rolling dunes of soft white sand and warm turquoise waters that meld into a spectacle of sunset, this plot of land had the makings of one of those proverbial perfect places in the sun. But childhood memories, utopia, or simply a genuine small town—pinnacles of place—are easier to imagine than to execute.

A BETTER WAY TO BUILD A TOWN

Throughout history, the natural landscape has given way to the built environment. Historic settlements and beloved towns have imparted a more benign and sympathetic occupation. More recently, American planners, architects, and developers relinquished the importance of human scale as the automobile became the driving force behind nameless and numbing suburban sprawl. Engaging neighborhoods and inviting urban spaces that had always provided a lively stage for interaction and memories were being irreversibly compromised.

Seaside is a negotiation of architecture in deference to the landscape. Its design springs naturally from the cultures, customs, and climate of the region. The homes and civic buildings engage their settings and provide meaningful uses. In the manner of admired civilizations and beloved settlements, Seaside is an augmentation of the land, a place where the act of building is an act of adoration, not a desecration.

For inspiration, Robert and Daryl looked to historic cities like Charleston and Savannah, small southern towns, villages along the Mediterranean Sea, and classic neighborhoods of the 1920s and '30s to determine why they have remained appealing. For more than two years, they allowed their ideas to develop slowly as they patiently set out to build something worthy of this special parcel of land Robert had inherited from his grandfather, J. S. Smolian.

In the process of formulating their ideas, Robert and Daryl met Andres Duany and Elizabeth Plater-Zyberk, a husband-and-wife team of architects practicing in Miami. The two couples shared philosophical dialogues and ambitious goals for a better way to build houses within the context of a new town.

At the time, there was no formula for what they intended to do. But they all had strong opinions about urban design, architecture, and what a town can and should be. The foursome set out on explorations together; sometimes cruising back roads in a red 1975 Pontiac convertible; other times venturing farther afield. These travels resulted in recollections, sketches, and photographs of historic places from DeFuniak Springs, Florida to Charleston to Martha's Vineyard to Portofino to Rome.

After visiting and literally measuring the details of small towns—the widths of streets and sidewalks, the heights of curbs and picket fences, the depths of front yards—they realized they had found the perfect model for planning a new community. Their goal was to revive the craft of building vernacular houses not in seclusion, but in the context of a small Southern town along the Gulf of Mexico. These inspirations and observations generated a town plan and a set of design guidelines and codes for building designed by the newly formed firm of DPZ & Company.

At this time, renowned urban theoretician Leon Krier was developing his own theories on classical town planning. Practicing in Europe, Leon Krier believed eighty acres was the optimal size for small towns. It was the distance someone would comfortably walk on a daily basis to work, to shops, to restaurants or, in Seaside's case, to the beach. The Davises met Leon Krier in 1980 and asked him to be involved. In exchange for consulting on the master plan, Leon Krier was offered a lot in Seaside, where the architect constructed a house on Tupelo Street, his first built work.

Seaside is one of those happy conjunctions of setting, timing, and talent. The original master plan and the way the town has changed over the years are reflections of this serendipitous collaboration.

"The earliest roots of a Seaside style actually evolved from our first house in the neighboring community of Grayton Beach," recalls Daryl Davis. "It was the most humble shack dating from the 1930s, but the structure had stood the test of time and weather and held up regally for all it went through over the years."

Before the first house was built in Seaside, Daryl began assembling vintage wicker furniture, sisal rugs, cotton curtains, scavenged lamps and other funky Florida finds to furnish their simple but dignified home. The look had a light touch, combining comfortable, upholstered sofas with lots of pillows, wood finished and pastel-colored walls, bouquets of flowers. It was comfortable and livable, and it had cachet. But it wasn't a deliberate effort to create a style or specific look. None of the furnishings was precious or pricey; everything was appropriate for the place and time. "The mood was no shoes, old wood that felt good under bare feet, and living in a bathing suit," says Daryl.

As Seaside's master plan was being finalized, the fledgling town had grown to include two modest bungalows on Tupelo Street and a beach pavilion built as a gateway to the beach. These early buildings—the Red House was the first sales office and the Yellow House was the home of Robert and Daryl—immediately set a framework for the architecture of the town and a tone for the relaxed approach to interior design that came to signify Seaside style. Prospective buyers were invited to "sit a spell" on the Davis's front porch or even join them for a dinner of fresh shrimp and home-grown tomatoes.

"These first houses required a great amount of thought," recalls Robert. "We were designing a home for ourselves as well as a model for the architecture and interior design of future houses." Now, more than twenty years after their construction, these two modest cottages and their simple furnishings seem so comfortable and unassumingly ensconced in their setting that it is hard to believe their design was a result of slow and thoughtful deliberations.

THE FOUNDATION

In the not so distant past, simple beach cottages responded intimately with their settings and the seasons. Seaside harkens to a time when towns and coastal resorts were crafted with care and concern for nature. Its town plan and individual houses were configured to create a real sense of community. Houses nod to the past with respect and wink at the present with open and inviting floor plans, cozy nooks with built-in bunks, and playful touches.

Seaside is based not on a single style, but on an attitude and an adaptation of the vernacular traditions—a synthesis of architectural traditions ranging from Florida Cracker to Carpenter Gothic to Victorian. By spelling out a vocabulary of materials and building types, Seaside's design guidelines foster coherence. Individual houses are encouraged to bear a strong family resemblance to one another—not to appear as identical twins.

From the beginning, Seaside property owners worked with individual architects and builders. Fresh interpretations of indigenous building techniques and traditional coastal architecture come together in the most original ways to embrace the glorious setting and recapture the essence of living along the water. Houses evolved over time to reflect changes in standing and situations.

The exuberant profiles of the houses are a genuine expression of varied inspirations and are decidedly appropriate to a relaxed, less restrained summer place. Shimmering canopies of pitched metal roofs crown colorful cottages animated with widow's walks, clerestories, wide overhangs, exposed rafters, and ample windows. Deep front porches instill a welcoming sense of scale, while traditional clapboard and board-and-batten siding reflect old-fashioned building techniques.

Reassuring and familiar, homes are an extension of community, not isolated structures in a remote setting. Eight distinct beach pavilions—each designed by a different architect—anchor the end of each street in Seaside to foster a sense of community and reinforce the importance of shared access to the beach.

Over the years, as individual designers explored the boundaries of the code an impressive range of architectural expressions emerged. As hoped, the design guidelines encouraged a compact urbanism based on human scale and proportion without dictating a deadening stylistic uniformity. Starting with Walter Chatham's dog trot cottage (page 160), the original plan was enlivened by energetically Modernist commercial buildings by Steven Holl (page 70), Machado and Silvetti Associates (page 88), and Deborah Berke.

The artist colony of Ruskin Place framed by townhouses designed by Alexander Gorlin, Walter Chatham and Lourdes Reynafarje further demonstrates flexibility inherent in the design codes and the authentic heterogeneity of the town. Three-story townhouses share party walls on twenty-one-foot lots, defining a distinctly urban space in contrast to the traditional designs of Seaside's early cottages. With shops on the ground floor and apartments above, Ruskin Place is a gracious, shared outdoor

room that has become a popular place for morning coffee, daily matches of the French lawn bowling game of *Pétanque*, or grand parties under a Moroccan tent.

THE LEGACY

Today, the concept of a planned community with a lively town center and pedestrian-friendly streets lined with wood-framed cottages with front porches hardly seems avant garde. However, in 1980 the notion was a radical approach to residential development—certainly along the beachfront property where the monolithic high-rise condominium was the conventional model. Unlike typical resort developments based on market research and consumer demand, Seaside started with memories of childhood summers along the Gulf and unbridled optimism for a better way of living along the water.

Seaside's first commercial ventures had humble beginnings. Its original Saturday Market was a glorified roadside stand with fresh shrimp, vegetables and fruits presented in colorful baskets and brightly colored tissue paper. "During our travels to coastal Mediterranean towns, we had marveled at outdoor marketplaces where commerce and community merged," recalls Daryl. "The forums and downtowns of these early settlements often started as simple canvas-shaded meeting spots."

The Seaside Saturday Market soon evolved into a series of permanent sheds with outdoor displays of simple cotton dresses, straw hats and baskets, beach cover-ups, and other colorful accessories, reminiscent of small-town farmers' markets or street bazaars in European villages. Later Daryl expanded the scope and selection, instilling a distinct personality and the name PER-SPI-CAS-ITY.

Seaside Town Center is an established retail destination with a lively collection of more than fifty shops, galleries, and restaurants, all within easy walking distance of each other. All shops in Seaside are privately owned and national chain outlets are not allowed. Seaside's own unique housewares store, Pizitz Home and Cottage, sets the standard for the Seaside style and created a unique version of "shabby chic" before shabby was chic. The shop continues to offer casual, sophisticated furnishings,

linens, tabletop accessories, and complete interior design services to homeowners furnishing their cottages.

A special alliance between architecture and the art of living was cultivated as the community continued to grow. Like a courthouse square or town green, Seaside's Central Square stands at the center of town and is defined by significantly larger three- and four-story mixed-use buildings. The semi-circular green space is the community's shared front lawn and hosts activities ranging from jazz concerts to wine festivals to community yard sales to performances by The Seaside Repertory Theatre.

In a short period of time, Seaside's fame spread through the architecture and design community and later the general public. In 1996, Seaside was selected as the location for the filming of *The Truman Show*. The movie stars Jim Carrey, a regular guy who is living a scripted life in an all-American town surrounded by actors and cameras that broadcast every minute of his days on television. The entire town of Seaside became a stage set. After filming was completed, location fees were donated to construct the Seaside Neighborhood School.

Articles about the town have appeared in professional journals, books, newspapers, and lifestyle travel magazines around the world. Yet Seaside is clearly more than an academic study. Seaside is founded on an ideal and stands as living proof of design principles based on humane scale and a shared sense of community. Seaside is profoundly appropriate for its time and place—a quality far more important than a formal architectural language or specific stylistic approach.

THE ESSENCE OF SEASIDE STYLE

Stylistic currents have ebbed and flowed since Seaside's founding in 1981. But Seaside style is not about a look or a fashion, or this year's color. Seaside style resonates with the joy of living along the water, of savoring the good things in life, of retreating from the worries of everyday.

The opportunities for fresh design and personal signatures are rarely greater than in a house on the beach. Many of Seaside's early houses buoyed their designers' reputation for inventiveness within an established framework.

Whatever the inspiration or direction of the winds of fashion, the houses of Seaside are firmly rooted in basic rules. Proportion, scale, unity, balance, and rhythm are constants. When any specific style or approach to design is regarded as a foundation rather than a formula, individuality abounds and style transcends fashion. Because style is so personal, the smallest details reflect personality and individuality. Graceful touches imbue everyday life with anticipation and exhilaration. Over the years, architects, designers, and residents have left their marks as homes and interiors have become more personalized.

If a village is a polite family of houses, Seaside has grown into an extended clan with more than its share of unique personalities. Many of the homes—and homeowners of Seaside—have strong opinions and they are not afraid to express them. Some of the homes are expressive and emotive; others are whimsical and carefree. Each in its own way is able to summon remnants of idyllic summer holidays of the past generate memories to carry into the future.

Yet for all the diversity of the houses of Seaside, there is a certainty of mutual respect and a shared appreciation of traditions that are understood by all. One common theme of these homes is the dual desire for a calm retreat and a sense of belonging —to get away from it all yet come together in a place of natural, architectural, and cultural significance.

In its emphasis on civility, optimism and escapism, Seaside is the living embodiment of an early twenty-first-century longing for a less complicated present. Life along the water revolves around a gracious spirit, abounding hospitality, and *joie de vivre*. The town of Seaside and this collection of houses are a shared celebration of those beliefs.

ARCHITECTURAL HARMONY

Rosewalk Cottages

Like a musical ensemble, Rosewalk is an intimate grouping of eleven cottages where all of the parts play in harmony to create an encompassing whole. Architects Melanie Taylor and Robert Orr orchestrated Seaside's design codes with grace and a wistful bow to a more romantic approach to architecture. Designed and built in the early 1980s when Seaside was in its formative stages, Rosewalk Cottages set the tone for the colors, forms, and detailing of many houses that followed in the early years.

Rosewalk stands as miniature urban enclave in a picturesque garden setting with each cottage a part of a complementary cast, and each contributing to a glorious larger composition. Rather than conformity, the individual cottages boast unique personalities and postures. Some are modest one-story cottages nestled among the trees, while others are two-story structures reaching for the sky and a view with observation towers and widow's walks. Pastel-colored facades layered in ornament animate the buildings from every angle.

Rosewalk's aura is similar to the historic coastal settlements of Oak Bluffs on Martha's Vineyard and Siasconset on Nantucket. Inspired by "stroll gardens" in the manner of picturesque English gardens, its individual houses and whimsical garden structures are carefully positioned to preserve the indigenous scrub oak and native plants. A series of footpaths and garden follies lend a coherent organization to the irregularly shaped site. Along the site's edges, three arched gateways signal the compound's network of paths and link them to the foot path system of Seaside.

The eleven cottages, ranging in size from 575 to one thousand square feet, were a refreshing new synthesis of a playful architectural exterior detailing and sunny whimsical interiors. Until that time, traditional

The cottages of Rosewalk set a precedent for Seaside with their engaging arrangement and quixotic gestures recalling beloved waterfront towns of the past. The first two-story houses completed in Seaside were located in Rosewalk. The added height and towers assure long views of the Gulf.

cottages typically featured chopped up interiors composed of a labyrinth of tiny rooms. In pleasing contrast, the Rosewalk Cottages are carefully scaled and proportioned. So rather than feeling cramped by their diminutive stature, both collectively and individually, they are immediately engaging.

Melanie Taylor relied on simple geometry, decorative detailing, and straightforward materials to give the ensemble of cottages their charm and character, yet the architect didn't merely appropriate historical form. The cottages engage a familiarity of the past while adopting contemporary patterns of living for their interiors.

"We looked to what has gone before and then let our creativity be influenced by the surroundings as freely as possible," says Daryl Davis, who designed the original interiors of several of the cottages, including Dreamsicle.

Each cottage of Rosewalk is different, yet all share tall ceilings and open floor plans promoting a sense of spaciousness. Their simplicity is the ultimate refinement. Walls disappear as the stairways, living and dining areas, and kitchen open one to each other. Deep covered porches and second-story verandahs double as living spaces and engage the deliciously green communal landscape. Everything about the cottages suggests repose.

Immediately embraced by the popular and professional press, Rosewalk illustrated early in the evolution of Seaside that a collection of houses and shared landscape designed and constructed in tandem with one another could be far richer than individual elements conceived in isolation.

"The original idea was a collection of dollhouses in a garden setting," explains Melanie. Twenty years later, a forest of scrub oak towers above the cottages as a protective canopy, further reinforcing the feeling of secrecy and playful mystery of Rosewalk.

Dreamsicle Cottage faces a sandy footpath, which provides a network for pedestrian traffic and connects the individual cottages of Rosewalk.

(Opposite) French doors open onto first and second floor porches, embracing the lush native landscape.

The cottage's organization offers dramatic surprises of light and views, while creating the most tempting spaces for relaxation.

21

Free-flowing spaces and a play of natural light infuse the relatively small cottages of Rosewalk with a sense of spaciousness and sophistication.

(Right)
Windows wrap a tower bedroom to offer commanding views.

early seaside

HOME-TOWN PRECEDENT

Davis
House

Standing guard next to the front doors, a trio of wooden sculptures by Wyman Pierce greets visitors to the Davis home.

Lush native vegetation offers a sheltering background for the deep front porch. An old-fashioned glider painted red and enlivened with black-and-white striped cushions combined with of a collection Adirondack chairs define a gracious and welcoming conversation area.

Every house tells a story about its inhabitants. Inherently coupled to their aspirations and aesthetics for the town of Seaside, the design of Daryl and Robert Davis's own home speaks volumes. A bit of page-turning memoirs of a small town coming of age on the Florida Panhandle.

In the early 1980s, Daryl and Robert lived in a humble cottage on Tupelo Street. Their modest Yellow House, as it was fondly called, was next to the real estate sales office. "Our home was always open to visitors and prospective buyers," recalls Daryl. "In addition to the architecture and interior design, we wanted to communicate the lifestyle we were living and reinforce the ultimate vision of Seaside."

The modest house was furnished with a mix of wooden rockers and wicker pieces, a picnic table, and a mix of casual fabrics including cotton duck, mattress ticking, and linens. Everything could be moved from the porch to living room

(Right)
The central dining room offers a tapestry of influences and materials. The room terminates in a cozy library nook accented with the same black-and-white tile as the kitchen. French doors on both walls open onto screened porches.

(Below)
The compact kitchen is arranged for efficiency. Easily accessed storage is positioned on either end. An antique apothecary cabinet is an attractive way to store and display accoutrements of a serious cook.

depending on the weather, and the décor showed just how easy life could be at the beach. "It was interesting to see how visitors responded to our home," recalls Daryl. "It wasn't contrived or condescending. It spoke to people on an emotional level and a lot of people embraced it immediately."

Five years into the process of building their town, Daryl and Robert embarked to build a larger house on a prominent site on Seaside Avenue, the town's residential promenade. Working with draftsman John Seaborn, the Davises designed their own 3,500-square-foot house. Robert concentrated on the architecture, while Daryl focused on the interiors and furnishings.

Determined and secure, Daryl and Robert sifted through forms of the past and icons of memory for a personal incorporation of borrowed motifs. The design of the house splices vernacular with contemporary sensibilities to form congenial spatial relationships. Inside and out, the house is endowed with humor and refinement without succumbing to excessive mannerism.

Naturally, the house respects the town's design guidelines. Its classical scale and proportions, axial arrangement, traditional clapboard siding, and double porches recall beloved historic homes of the South. To interrupt slightly the formal symmetry, the front door is set off center and opens directly into a large living room that runs along the length of the house.

The sparely furnished master bedroom creates a mood of serenity. Soft colors, natural woods, and a modicum of accessories enhance the ordered calm.

(Opposite)
The centerpiece of the outdoor dining room is a sturdy farm table with red legs and an unpainted tabletop. A side table painted a lively shade of blue and a primitive armoire stand along the interior wall protected from the elements. The picket fence motif echoes picket fences that define the community.

The drama of expansive spaces and deft handing of natural materials unfolds immediately. Woods of varying tones and finishes, including maple floors, birch paneling, and fir trim, add warmth.

Both Daryl and Robert love every aspect of food and the table, so the kitchen occupies the literal and figurative heart of the house. "We moved into the house when our son Micah was one year old," recalls Daryl. "We really are a family who lives in the kitchen and we wanted a space to be comfortable and convenient for both intimate dinners and entertaining larger groups."

All rooms radiate from an efficient galley kitchen—compact but outfitted with all the tools of a serious cook—set perpendicular to the double-height dining room. Glossy, four-inch-square, black-and-white tiles introduce a contemporary touch in the kitchen, and a cozy reading nook is set at the opposite end of the dining room. This impressive double-height space identifies the distribution of rooms on both the first and second floor.

Two sets of French doors along both walls of the central gathering space allow the boundaries between indoors and outdoors to disappear. Screen porches along both sides of the house are comfortable most of the year round and reflect the relaxed charm of the surrounding native landscape. A thick crown of wisteria transforms a large open deck into a cloistered outdoor room and shades the adjoining porch, outfitted with a sturdy farm table for al fresco dining.

Like the town of Seaside, Daryl and Robert's own house is a triumph of style and substance. But Daryl is the first to admit that she didn't consciously set out to create a Seaside style or to influence anyone. "I did hope to match the intelligence and logic of the town plans and architecture with an integrity in terms of lifestyle and attention to all the little details that are so important," says Daryl. Along the way, through shops like Pizitz Home & Cottage and PER-SPI-CAS-ITY, Daryl established a trademark imagery for Seaside, and a relaxed approach to interior design.

"We didn't really invent anything," says Daryl. "We took a tried-and-true framework and made it more colorful, congenial, interesting, and noticeable. Over the years, people have come and experienced Seaside on many levels. By embracing it, they are constantly reinforcing the original vision." At the end of the day, that's what Seaside Style is really all about.

SMALL ONLY IN STATURE

Honeymoon Cottages

Pure might be one way to describe this series of precise and repetitive little cottages along the Gulf of Mexico. Fondly called Honeymoon Cottages, they stand just behind the primary dune line as a tangible representation of a fleeting perfection without pretension.

Their name, as well as their diminutive massing, was inspired by the so-called "Honeymoon Cottage" that Thomas Jefferson lived in for two years with his new bride as he constructed Monticello. "Jefferson's historic outbuilding settles into the hillside, allowing the structure to appear as one story from above on the lawn and a full two stories from down the hill," explains architect Scott Merrill. "Robert Davis wanted to create that same illusion for a series of narrow and low cottages right on the beach."

Two groupings of six identical cottages are nestled between Seaside's tall natural dune line and a sand footpath that runs the length of the town parallel to the shoreline. The contour of the site delivers the same visual effect, allowing Seaside's Honeymoon Cottages to appear as one story from the beach below, minimizing their impact.

Although comprising only one thousand square feet including porches, the cottages demand attention—maybe for the refinement of their familiar Greek Revival-inspired forms, their confident dead-pan repetition, or the sheer glory of their setting. "Seaside was conceived as a town where certain Gulf coast residential building types would be repeated," says Scott. "A reasonable amount of repetition was imagined to be visually desirable and financially necessary. The Honeymoon Cottages ennoble necessary repetition."

This fetching mix of modesty and monumentality is repeated inside. The Honeymoon Cottages assert a spatial economy through a logical arrangement of spaces. Simplicity is their essence. Pine floors, whitewashed wooden walls, crisp white linens, and rockers on the porch. The luxury is the spectacle, the serenity, the sun, the shade.

The first floor is devoted to a spacious bath with a tiled shower big enough for two and a pleasant bedroom that opens onto a private screened porch. Billowing curtains grant privacy for the generous porch and a hot tub.

A cozy stairway winds its way up to the second floor where the living room takes full advantage of the view. The interiors are deliberately cool and monochromatic, always striking a pleasant balance with the intimate scale of the rooms and the infinity of the outside world. Sunlight cascades into the cottage, constantly changing the mood of the rooms. At high noon a turquoise Gulf shimmers, while later in the day, as the sun dips toward the horizon, waves glisten with shades of gold and pink.

(Page 33)
From East Ruskin Pavilion, the three original Honeymoon Cottages establish a strong sense of classical repetition along the beach.

(Opposite, Top)
On the second floor, the seascape commands attention in the intimate living room. Traditional double-hung windows frame succulent views of white sand and turquoise water.

(Above)
The ground floor screen porch boasts an oversized hot tub. Scrub oak surround the porch in an envelope of natural privacy. Bedrooms are located on the ground floor. Cotton sailcloth curtains dance in the breeze.

Helvie Cottage

From the street, there is nothing extraordinary about Diane Helvie's diminutive beach cottage. Its simple metal roofline, operable shutters, and wraparound porches closely follow the traditional cracker cottages built generations ago in small towns and waterfront settlements of the Panhandle. Sights, sounds, and smells of the house harken to a simpler time. A gentle clap of the screen doors announces the comings and goings of family and friends. The clatter of raindrops on a metal roof interrupts a lazy Saturday afternoon. Saw palmetto branches rustle in the distance. Whiffs of honeysuckle and Confederate jessamine mingle with breezes coming off the Gulf.

The first house completed on the west side of Seaside, Diane's bungalow is more akin to the early houses on Tupelo Street than its larger neighbors that followed on Odessa Street. Built by Suellen Hudson, the house was her fifth variation on a theme of the archetypal cracker cottage. (See her own house on page 118) The house occupies a large lot, and the placement of its relatively compact footprint creates a generous side yard to maximize outdoor living. Colors of varying shades of green live harmoniously with the magnolias, scrub oaks, and sago palms.

Step through the double screen doors and into a deep front porch and the magic of the house unfolds. Interior spaces are arranged in a straightforward manner with a continuous living and dining space at the center of the house, yet the soaring ceiling and exposed beams add volume and instill a sense of drama. The walls never close in on this relatively small house. French doors in the living room and each of the bedrooms swing out to savor the great outdoors.

The selection and placement of furnishings and accessories that are scaled precisely—sometimes overscaled—add to this illusion of spaciousness. Drawing from a fresh and lively palette of materials and fixtures, a sumptuous marble mantel counters the natural wood floors and painted paneled walls. A colorful antique French poster grabs attention above the mantle and a glorious chandelier accentuates the room's tall ceiling.

An efficient galley kitchen is tucked just off the living room, conveniently located for entertaining—either for a dinner party for four inside or a larger group dining al fresco. Three tiny but inviting bedrooms, each with a bath, anchor the corners of the house. The heart of the house, however, is the fourteen-foot-deep screen porch that wraps around the front and side of the house accommodating a grand outdoor dining room and corner conversation area. An equally deep porch extending along the rear of the house affords the two back bedrooms a private outdoor retreat.

The patina of age the house has already acquired is a function of its time-tested forms and materials as well as Diane and her son Stuart Bell's flair for life. "The décor takes its cues from New Orleans, Provence, Aspen, and casual beach cultures," says Stuart. "We love to travel and acquire things as reminders of the places we visit. It is in constant evolution and not concerned with being perfect."

The house works because it is designed for easy living— colors are warm and inviting, the furniture is soft and comfortable. "I like to surround myself with beautiful things that are utilitarian— like using my silver and porcelain every day. I can't concern myself about what's fragile," says Diane. "This home is casual yet sophisticated, and to be lived in without worrying."

This is a special Seaside cottage. Much like a piece of crystal, this home is alluring and a bit mysterious, engagingly transparent yet designed to be faceted with various surprises. It's neither the grandest architectural statement nor the most extravagant view—but it has all the allure one could ever want in its detail, warmth, and charm of a house by the sea.

(Previous Page)
A common-sense response to the climate and context, a landscaped terrace runs along the south side of the house. The intimate garden room accommodates a cozy conversation area and outdoor dining space; a gate allows access from the street and connects to the side porch as well as the back porch and a more private rear terrace.

(Right)
The colors and forms of the house and the matter-of-fact landscape seem inevitable—as though they have been there for ages and they belong.

Diane's artistic arrangement of antiques and accessories weaves a unifying thread inside and out. An antique marble fireplace, a gilded mirror and an oversized French poster create a bold focus.

A recessed alcove accommodates a double bed. Built-in bookshelves and wall-mounted reading lamps make the most of limited space. The ornate mirror adds a sense of drama.

Inside and out, every corner of the house is filled with global souvenirs.

Outdoor dining is an everyday occurrence in all four seasons on the deep side porch. The sturdy marble and cast iron table lends old-world charm.

43

strictly personal

THROUGHLY
MODERN
MANNERS

Dowler
House

44

"A house, more than any other building type, is free to be idiosyncratic," says architect Rafael Pelli. "And a home should be a portrait of its owners." Marsha and David Dower are clearly reflected in their Seaside abode. There's not an excess of clamor in the house; there is an abundance of personal resolve.

The first impression of the Dowler home, like many houses in Seaside, presents an unassuming face to the outside world. The transition from the street to the inner sanctum is rewarding, either via the wide front porch to the foyer or through the back gate that opens directly into their private garden.

"David had clear intentions and a particular vision for the house," recalls Raphael, who partnered with Houston architect Nonya Grenader on the design. They refined the traditions of modernism to elemental simplicity in terms of forms, while transforming materials and surfaces through the exploration of new treatments and techniques.

"Basically, we exploded a large program and reassembled the parts into a main house and two freestanding guest houses, giving each a private entrance and identity," says the architect. This arrangement allows Marsha and David to be alone in the main house or they can open up one or both of the guest houses for entertaining large groups of friends and family.

A double lot accommodated this contemporary take on the traditional Charleston Single House. Conceived as a polite gathering of three related pavilions, the compound frames a cloistered courtyard, animated with stepped terraces and lush native landscaping designed by Randy Harelson. Textures, fragrances, and forms of the indigenous plants enhance the definition and appeal of the open decks and covered porches.

The entire exterior including trim is painted what David calls "vanilla white." The chaste color—which was not part of Seaside's approved palette—announces the pure form of the building and sets it off against the green landscape and blue sky.

Inside, a contemporary response provides open spaces flowing one to another. Architectural details—rather than solid walls—define the functions of these rooms. Issues of style are peripheral at best. A sense of restraint is the architectural order.

Because the architecture has such an understated character, Marsha and David let it set the tone for the interiors. Throughout the house, the design, restrained and pared down, is the perfect background for David's collection of fine art photography. "I started acquiring black-and-white photography in 1973," recalls David. "It was one of the few art forms that were affordable at the time."

Primarily water or beach themes simply framed, the collection of photographs is the focal point of the neutral interiors and understated furnishings. The living room has an airy spaciousness, yet even in this most formal room of the house, the mood is relaxed and spare. A trio of photographs by Sally Gall rests comfortably above an unassuming sofa slip covered in cotton duck. *Sorry* by Sally Mann commands the prominent position above the fireplace.

The spirit of the house converges in the kitchen and dining room, a large open space with equally tall ceilings and exposed beams. The horizontal painted paneling is repeated in the cabinets. Details are crisp and carefully crafted with a promise to stand up to the test of time. In keeping with the unadorned feel, windows on the second floor are left bare upstairs. The deep side porch along the west side of the house offers privacy and assures that the light is always balanced, never glaring.

There's nothing pretentious about Marsha and David Dowler's Seaside home. Although the house possesses a grace and elegance in its architectural aspirations, the appeal lies in its simplicity and rambling spirit. First-time visitors and old family friends move about the compound with the same of sense of belonging. But more appropriately, it is a home that reflects its owners in a mirror as large as life.

(Previous Page)   Although inspired by courtyard houses of Charleston or New Orleans, this house offers a decidedly contemporary twist. In the private courtyard, sun and shade provide variety throughout the day.

(Right)   The Spartan elegance of this home is less about objects and furnishings than it is about photography and a philosophical approach to life. Stacked windows facing the courtyard accentuate the exposed beams and tall ceilings.

Interior walls are clad with wide horizontal paneling painted white, a fresh abstraction of a treatment typical of early Florida houses.

A large round table anchors the sunny dining room. Matching blond wood chairs and bar stools reinforce a sense of continuity between adjoining spaces.

AN ENCORE PERFORMANCE

Hoover House

Step onto the porch and into the front door of Mary Moore Hoover's Seaside home and enter her own special world. It's a place she has deftly tailored to suit her lifestyle and to reflect a distinct personal style. And it's not the first Seaside house where she's left her signature.

Mary Moore Hoover with her son, Craige Hoover, and her mother and brother were one of the first families of Seaside, building a shared compound on Tupelo Street. A few years later, she ventured to Ruskin Place for a home of her own, and worked with Alexander Gorlin on the design of one of his five distinctive townhouses that define the park.

Always eager for a new challenge, she was ready a few years later when she spotted a classically inspired house on West Ruskin Street. Designed by Ken Isaacs, the house had more architectural stature than actual square footage.

Mary Moore was in the process of relocating to Seaside full-time and she knew she would need more space. With a vision, Mary Moore transformed the jewel of a house—albeit a bit impractical for full-time use—into an utterly livable and likable home.

To respect the home's architectural integrity and unique details, Mary Moore retained the front facade with its double front porches and extended the house to the rear with two bays repeating the symmetry and rhythm of the original structure. Large windows along the original rear elevation were removed and reused in the new composition.

This opened up the downstairs to allow for two guest suites, each with a private bath. Existing architectural features, including changes in elevation, archways, and interior Doric columns, retain the spirit of the original design. Upstairs, the added square footage transformed a tiny studio into an expansive loftlike space measuring twenty-five by twenty-five feet. By far the largest room in the house, the new space contains the master bed, a claw-tooth tub, home office, and a gracious conversation area focused on a new fireplace.

(Previous Page)
*The home's corner location on East Ruskin and Route 30-A boasts wonderful views
of the pavilion and Gulf beyond. A trio of French doors on double front porches swings
open to diminish the distinction between inside and out.*

*(Above)   The expanded master suite offers a distinctive new character, strong enough to
meld the classical origins with practical adaptations to become a remarkable place of its own.*

*(Right)   Sturdy pillars indicate where the original house ended. Floor-to-ceiling fixed windows along the rear elevation
were recycled, flooding the expanded bedroom with natural light and creating two new bays along the back of the house.*

Practicality and a bit of sentiment, as much as style, determine the choice of finishes and furnishings. Many of the prominent pieces of furniture are family antiques handed down for generations. Fabrics, finishes, and furniture are another way Mary Moore weaves her personality and incorporates flexibility into her very personal master suite. A mix of animal-inspired prints, bamboo blinds, and an Alpaca rug and bed throw counter the four wing chairs slip-covered in simple cotton duck. The fireplace is clad with Peruvian slate. As practical touches, a Chinese panel sets off the antique tub or can be moved to serve as a screen, and a large armoire delineates and provides out of view storage.

There's never a short supply of visitors and activities in this Seaside home. And entertaining seems effortless for Mary Moore no matter what the occasion. Her son, Craige Hoover, is the founder of the Seaside Repertory Theatre. Throughout the year, the house is often a venue for opening and closing theater parties as well as holiday gatherings for family and friends.

Conventional wisdom says that everyone congregates in the kitchen at a party. Not at Mary Moore Hoover's Seaside home. When the claw-foot tub is filled with Champagne and there's a fire roaring in the master suite's fireplace, the action gravitates in that direction. By the end of the night, everyone ends up in the bedroom.

(Opposite)
Antiques and new pieces mingle comfortably, as if they've known each other for years. A round antique table counters the clean lines of a compact galley kitchen.

(Right)
Architectural details like the Doric columns and archways retain the charm of the original design. The antique linens and iron bed belonged to Mary Moore's great grandmother.

strictly personal
FLASHBACK TO OLD FLORIDA

Moore Cottage

In the not so distant past of the 1940s and '50s, simple cottages along waterfronts from Maine to Miami to Montecito responded intimately to their settings and the seasons. Step through the front door of Margee and Bill Moore's little corner of Seaside into a world where memory takes form.

"I grew up in Northern California and our family spent our summers along the Monterey Bay," recalls Margee. "As our daughter got older, I knew we had to have a beach house of our own."

Now settled in Tennessee after a military career that took them around the world, Margee and Bill determined the Florida Panhandle was a logical destination. From their first visit to Seaside, they saw it was different from other resorts. It is a real town that elicits memories of halcyon days of summer before high-rise condominiums, air conditioning, and traffic congestion. The Moores also loved the fact that everything was within easy walking distance of the town center. When they found a cozy bungalow close to the Gulf, they knew they had found their new home at the beach.

A cordial peaked gable roof animated with fanciful wooden fretwork and a deep front porch defines the house. The gingerbread ornament and forms in themselves conjure up storybook scenes of a grandmother's house. Exterior Bermuda shutters painted a cheerful shade of teal green are fitted with fixed horizontal louvers designed to diffuse sunlight inward while offering a sense of privacy and hurricane protection.

The familiar Florida forms continue to resonate in the ebullient interiors. In the one large living and dining area, a hollowed up ceiling expresses the volume of early beach houses where light and air were encouraged to move within. An L-shaped counter defines the kitchen—deep enough for casual dining while allowing the cook to always be part of the action.

The home meshes comfort and creativity, sentiment with eccentricity, all the while reveling in the flavors of old Florida and Cracker-style architecture. Margee goes brighter, airier, and funkier and makes sure everything is mixed, not matched. Colors are deliberately cool and faded,

striking a pleasing balance with the intensity of the outdoors. The interiors appear as if they had fallen together contentedly over the years. Kitschy Florida plates, pink flamingos, painted conchs, cypress-knee lamps—Marge left no shell unturned in her search for memorabilia of a time not to be forgotten—at least at her Seaside home.

A central hallway connects the home's three-bedrooms and a cloistered garden terrace. Tucked behind the main house amid a lush native landscape is a secluded guesthouse for visiting friends. Designed by architect Eric Watson, the cottage has as much pizzazz as the main house. Sea-foam green walls instill a calming repose in the petite upstairs bedroom. "We wanted to create a dollhouse-like cottage where we would like to be guests," says Margee. Visitors appreciate the effort. There's a strong decorative flavor, but comfort is always foremost.

The collections keep growing with additions from a multitude of sources. The Moores are always stopping at antique shops and flea markets along the way. "Once we found a wonderful piece in a shop in Florala," recalls Margee. "It wouldn't fit in the car, but our daughter Allyson was coming in a few days and brought it down." Friends who visit often leave gifts in keeping with the spirit of the place.

There's no right way or wrong way to decorate a house at the beach. It's the passion and spirit behind the effort that becomes the memory. Like so many of the very personal homes along the tree-lined streets of Seaside, this house embodies the reveries of long ago summers by the sea, whether the Atlantic, Pacific or the Gulf. The Moores have created a place that feels familiar and lovingly cared-for. But it's as much about looking forward as looking backward. And it is sure to be a place where family traditions will continue for generations.

(Previous Page)
An ample supply of gingerbread trim, a friendly gable roof, and a welcoming front porch offer a taste of wonderful things to come.

(Right)
Sunlight cascades into the living room. Vintage floral fabrics, hordes of shells, and souvenirs give the interiors a look of old Florida.

The cozy guest cottage packs a lot of personality in a small space. An antique wicker fainting couch tucks within a sunny bay. The upstairs bedroom has its own balcony.

Vignettes encourage closer examinations and illicit memories of a simpler time along the coast.
A guest bedroom is dressed in vintage bedspreads with verdant swirls of hibiscus blooms and tiger lily leaves.

SHIPSHAPE BY THE SEA

Callaway
House

Close proximity to the water is a luxury to be exploited. Debra and Mark Callaway's house revels in the immeasurable possibilities of the sights and sounds of the Gulf of Mexico. An effervescent combination of purpose and delight, their house was designed by Tampa architect Don Cooper. It commands a sense of serenity and order that would be proper on a grand sailing ship, and its gracious decks and decor exudes an open invitation to linger, to relax, and to enjoy.

Water and sailing are the unifying themes of the house. "Mark's father had raced sailboats all over the world and the entire family loves boats," explains Don. "The nautical references struck a chord." Don develops variations on this theme for both the interiors and exterior; like a well-composed piece of music, the house unfolds with consistency and elements of surprises along the way.

Beckoning visitors, the street facade abstracts characteristics of Greek Revival with stout Doric columns supporting an extended portico. "We wanted to create an impression of a house hunkering down to face the elements," says Don. Seaside codes mandated a maximum height of twenty-two feet. To counter the low profile, eyebrow windows punctuate the roofline with playful winks to both the street side and Gulf side.

A beach house demands that every space is designed for everyday living. "From our first meeting, Don was always questioning, always listening, always thinking about creating a house for the way we live," says Debra. In terms of materials and detailing, the house is

(Pages 62 - 63)
Nautical elements and sailing references are strong, yet this house is clearly rooted to the land. The house embraces the friendly sand foot paths that criss-cross the town of Seaside.

(Left)
Windows along three elevations of the large kitchen and dining room acknowledge the breathtaking beauty that lies beyond the walls. Mahogany ceilings and heart-pine floors create a pleasant counterpoint to sunny and open spaces, allowing every room in the house to feel good whatever the season.

MORNING STAR
TRANSPACIFIC RECORD HOLDER
LOS ANGELES-HONOLULU 1949-1955
LOS ANGELES · TAHITI 1961

MEN AND SHIPS AROUND CAPE HORN

(Page 66)
The succinct palette allows colors and materials to flow seamlessly throughout
the house from the central living room to the adjoining master bedroom.

(Page 67)
The craftsmanship continues into the master bedroom. Identical built-in desks frame either side of the fireplace.
The painting is of the "Morning Star," the boat that Mark's father raced.

(Above) The glory of the house opens up with the central living room, which holds the Callaways' precisely placed collections of sailing artifacts, paintings, and trophies from past races. A generous L-shape built in sofa defines the room. A pair of swivel chairs allows for flexibility to focus on the conversation area or out to the view.

(Opposite) In the master bedroom, the décor respects the miraculous spirit of this place without confining it within a historical moment. Vintage racing photographs and a silver challis from of Mark's father's triumphs on the water, grace the living room.

crafted and outfitted as soundly as a sailing ship yacht. "We also insisted on the hardiest materials we could find from top to bottom," says Debra. The roof is solid leaded copper, and floors are heart pine. Doors and windows are mahogany. The crowning touch is the ceiling, crafted of honed tongue-in-groove mahogany and exposed trusses.

"All the cabinets and most of the furniture were designed and crafted by Burrell Elliot and Stan Ray, true artists and master builders," adds Debra. Everything is either built-in or bolted down, as if to protect them in a sudden squall: the dining room table and benches; the U-shaped sectional sofa oriented for front row seats of the view of the Gulf; even the master bed is secured. Clever storage occupies wall compartments and floor hatches. Outside decks are teak. There's nothing fussy—the house is at once shipshape and sophisticated.

The floor plan is equally straightforward, defining the individuality of each room. The main living spaces and the master bedroom are located on the second floor taking full advantage of the extra volume of the roofline and views out. Downstairs bedrooms are designed with family and guests in mind. The children's wing accommodates two large bedrooms with four built-in berths each. "We wanted plenty of beds so each of our four children could all bring a friend at the same time," says Debra. There's also a gracious guest suite for visiting adults.

Any beach house worth its salt has an outdoor shower. Both ends of the house are dominated by a large outdoor shower. Curtains of striped sailcloth billow in the breeze as a decorative element, while offering privacy. Each shower has double doors that open directly into the downstairs bathrooms.

There's an elegance in how the parts and materials of this house come together, retaining the integrity of each. Forms, materials, and themes are repeated, but the duplication is reassuring, not a series of overworked clichés. The Callaway home is a firmly grounded vessel, yet it happily floats in its own world with a charted path always pointing towards the welcomed distractions and pleasant diversions of life along the water.

A TURNING OF THE TIDE

Dreamland Heights

Some rock stars fondly recall their early days playing in joints off the beaten track. Others maintain a more selective memory. But loyal fans can always recant tales of artists' performances before their big break. Aficionados' best recollections usually involve a dozen or so nonchalant patrons in a dark smoky bar in a town like Lubbock or Lexington.

Seaside is a long way from New York or Los Angeles. But in the 1980s, a fair share of rising architectural talent was finding the town an amenable venue for their brand of creativity. Fifteen years before *Time* magazine named Steven Holl "architect of the year" in 2001, he was designing a commercial building for Seaside, the Haight-Ashbury of New Urbanism.

The gig was a four-story, hybrid building composed of shops, offices, and apartments. It was by far the largest building at the time and the first permanent building to be constructed along Seaside's ambitious Central Square. The building was christened Dreamland Heights by Robert Davis, as a tribute to his grandfather, J. S. Smolian, and his decades-old scheme for a summer camp for employees of his department store, Pizitz, on the land that eventually became Seaside.

From the beginning Seaside codes were never intended to dictate a particular style or historical replication, but rather to encourage regional building traditions to infuse coherence, cohesion, and a strong sense of place.

In designing Dreamland Heights, Steven Holl readily acknowledged the rationale of Seaside's urbanistic dictates, as well as the predetermined footprint and requirements for an arcade with storefronts for ground-floor retail. He was undaunted by prescribed design covenants that other architects had seen as restrictive, and went about designing his own concurrent architectural order. All said and done, Dreamland Heights possesses a bold swagger, purged of historical sentimentality.

Rising to seventy-five feet in height, the building is organized as a two-story base containing shops and offices. The building's exterior abstract massing and unadorned angularity is a subtle hint of what takes place within. An unassuming entrance lobby accessing second-story offices

(Page 71)
Vibrant and kinetic, Dreamland Heights and the adjacent Modica Market
generate urbanity along the southeastern edge of Central Square.

(Opposite)
In the house of the mathematician everything is slightly askew.
The stairway to the second level projects on an angle over the bathroom.

(Above)
Large windows of the "boisterous" apartments afford warm afternoon light.

via a stairway and an elevator, clad in a patina finished with perforated bronze panels, indicate that Steven Holl's Modernist sensibilities prevail throughout.

An integral part of the architecture and interior design, Steven Holl composed an imaginary story line about a "society of strangers" who would inhabit the building. To accommodate these restless souls, the building's form splits into eight apartments, arranged as east- and west-facing blocks on the upper two floors. The apartments share a central courtyard on the upper two floors.

Those facing the setting sun and Central Square are rooms for boisterous types, late risers who enjoy watching the action of the town center and amphitheatre and savoring the sunset. These five feature two levels connected with a spiral stairway. The living room ceilings echo the prominent curve of the building's barrel-vaulted roof.

Facing east, to the rising sun are three apartments, designed for an imaginary tragic poet, a musician and a mathematician. Each is furnished and finished accordingly. In the house of the musician, light is cast down from the corner windows on the upper level. A black plaster wall slips from the lower to the upper floor enhancing the flowing nature of the space.

Dreamland Heights received rave reviews from the design press in late 1980s. (It was featured as a cover story on Progressive Architecture and winner of a National AIA award.) The building stands as concrete proof of the diversity possible within the Seaside design codes. It also is a testament to another aspect of creating a real town. To rephrase Kevin Costner's line from the movie *Field of Dreams,* Dreamland Heights proves that "if you build it, they will have an opinion." And that's no small accomplishment for a structure, style notwithstanding.

The penthouse apartments share a third-floor courtyard with views of the water. The rooftop terrace of one apartment takes a decidedly fresh twist with vernacular precedents. The abstracted trellis evokes a modern stance without sacrificing the timeless tradition of relaxing in a hammock.

LOFTY IDEAL

urban by the sea

Forsythe Townhouse

Creative expressions are infinite. This townhouse revels in the artistic attitudes of its owners Mary Florence and Bill Forsythe and the contemporary sensibilities of its architect Walter Chatham. As the first building completed in Ruskin Place, the house immediately set a lively contemporary aesthetic for Seaside's most urban neighborhood.

The Forsythes, like many Seaside residents, didn't come to Florida looking to build a second home. "We came down for a long weekend," recalls Mary Florence. "After our first morning on the beach we were so enamored with the place, we bought property that afternoon." When it came to selecting an architect, they wanted a designer who shared their artistic objectives and outlook on life. "We were intrigued the first time we saw Walter Chatham's dog trot house," says Mary Florence. As it turned out, Walter had recently purchased property along Ruskin Place. "We told him we had a very limited budget," recalls Mary Florence. "But Walter agreed to design our house because he said he wanted 'practice' before he designed his own townhouse."

Financial limitations force you to be creative and often prompt the most innovation solutions. "The second floor above the kitchen was removed to save money," says Mary Florence. "And it's one of the best aspects of the design."

The arrangement of rooms is a straightforward response to the dictates of the footprint and height of the building. Every room in the house is interchangeable except the kitchen. Originally, the ground-floor room facing the square served as an art school in summer months for visitors to Seaside. Now, it's the living room.

Likewise, stairways that could have been viewed as necessities taking up valuable square footage become the defining aesthetic. Their raw structure with simple wood risers and taut cable railings instills a dramatic industrial image, almost poetic in its essential representation of form.

Instead of using solid walls to separate the kitchen and the living room, Walter incorporated a central core containing service functions including bathrooms, storage, and mechanical equipment. This internal

76

(Page 77)
Facing Ruskin Place, the townhouse's concrete structure is softened with
corrugated wood panels, green trim and doors, and clinging wines.

(Opposite)
The living room's symmetrical paneled doors swing open to take advantages of the park.
The transoms repeat the square pattern and accentuate the height of the room.

(Above)
Unfinished concrete-block walls are painted a creamy white and continue the industrial loft feel in the living room.
Furnishings are a mix of overstuffed upholstered pieces for real comfort, vintage butterfly chairs with well-worn leather seating,
and a custom coffee table crafted of copper and stone.

(Opposite)
The thoughtful placement of art, such as one of Mary Florence's sculptures at
the top of the stairway, creates interesting vistas through the house.

(Above)
The master suite occupies the top floor overlooking Ruskin Place. Salvaged goods create artistic furniture.
Mary Florence combined a steel slab and two square pillars from a junk yard to make the dressing table.

core rises through the house and eventually pops up out of the roof as a high-tech widow's walk. As a result, interior walls are basically nonexistent, except for this core. Structural concrete block walls are left exposed and painted a soothing shade of creamy white.

The kitchen cabinets are another clever response to the limited funds. To counter the slick surfaces and industrial stainless steel appliances, builder Michael Warner crafted the rolling kitchen cabinets out of a persimmon tree that had fallen on his property in the midst of construction. The kitchen features commercial storage racks in lieu of traditional cabinets; the kitchen sink is set in a poured concrete bed and supported by concrete legs wrapped in steel.

Judiciously sprinkled throughout the industrial environment are flourishes of a more artistic and ethereal kind thanks to both Mary Florence and Bill. As varied as their tastes, possessions, and artwork, the Forsythes blend them harmoniously. Thanks to a natural gift of visualization, the rooms always look right. Nothing matches, but everything seems perfectly at home.

Mary Florence's artistic influences can be found in the decorating touches as well. Without the luxury of plush materials, paint served as an important decorative element. What appears to be wallpaper in the center core of the house is actually metallic aluminum paint that Forsythe sponged over a flat gray.

"Designing a house was a satisfying experience, thanks to our relationship with Walter and his family," Bill Forsythe said. "Walter was energized by our program. He took the code and designed something unabashedly contemporary yet timeless and perfectly suited for us."

The house is a masterful manipulation of vertical and axial layering to create views to the outdoors both up through the open stairways and out through adjoining spaces on every floor. As a result, the house succeeds in being intimate yet intimately connected to the park. "We really consider Ruskin Place to be a shared outdoor living room," says Mary Florence. Not surprising, their artist touches are not limited to the confines of their four walls. Bill created the two large metal sculptures of a man and woman, framing the entrance to the park.

LIVING ABOVE THE STORE

Baratta/
Holtermann
Townhouse

The old-fashioned concept of living above the store has been revived with imaginative results at Quincy's, located along the entrance to Seaside's lively artist colony, Ruskin Place. Rather than relying on the more romantic notions of vernacular traditions and coastal bungalows, architect Lourdes Reynafarje of Kiara Designs summons urban aesthetics for a toy and arts supply emporium owned by native New Yorkers Dorothy Baratta and Cliff Holtermann.

The couple was immediately intrigued by Seaside's cohesive town plan and engaging architecture. "The first weekend we visited in the late 1980s we bought property and soon commissioned Deborah Berke to design a cottage," recalls Dorothy. "By the time we had completed our first house, we had a new appreciation of architecture."

As Seaside evolved, Dorothy and Cliff were drawn to the energy and density of the growing town center and the live-work units defining Ruskin Place. They soon purchased another lot. "This is as urban as Florida gets, and we love it," says Dorothy.

Design codes dictate ground-floor retail with apartments above for this section of the growing town. "From the beginning, we assumed we would lease the retail space, rent the second-floor apartment, and use the third floor as our vacation home," recalls Dorothy. As part of the process, they developed a concept for a ground-floor shop. "We were so impressed with our ideas for the store that we decided to establish a major business with the cavalier attitude of someone setting up a lemonade stand," she adds.

At once contemporary and contextual, the building from the lively ground-floor shop to the third-floor apartment responds to the modernist tenet of efficiency and elegance by straightforward means and materials. The architect chose a hard, steel-troweled concrete exterior and the overscaled galvanized steel brackets to evoke the industrial sense of the maritime warehouses of the past. Following this premise, the store and residence appear as a transformation of an abandoned shell to vibrant spaces adapted to a variety of new functions.

Patterns of circulation and the rhythmic arrangement of spaces are continuous and constant. The three-story building features a front and a back stairway, which carve out a pair of light wells with corner windows to bring natural light into the mid-block townhouse. This arrangement also allows the second floor to function as two separate rental units.

Throughout, concrete floors, ceilings, walls, and countertops provide a bold, yet neutral backdrop for colorful accents of tile, eclectic furnishings, and art. For the owners' third-floor apartment, designer Kris Childs used a few large pieces of furniture to define the functions of the loftlike main living space. An antique farm table easily accommodates ten for dinner. An intimate conversation area focuses on a fireplace. Suspended shelving offers a subtle definition between the kitchen and living area, while providing decorative storage.

Modern design is easy to embrace when things are paired down to their simplest elements. "Lourdes created a space that is as elemental, raw, and sensuous as the beach, without sacrificing comfort and practicality," says Dorothy. "It is a home that has tested as well for quiet meditation, romantic encounters, and raucous parties."

(Previous Page)
The master suite is an oasis of restraint with tall windows and minimalist details.

(Opposite)
Quincy's array of toys and arts supplies enlivens the shop's entrance. Stainless steel railings and industrial beams define the second-floor balcony.

(opposite)
One corner of the master suite accommodates a deep soaking tub set with a curving wall
of pour-in-place concrete. A recessed fireplace anchors the opposite wall.

(Above)
An L-shaped counter defines the compact and efficient kitchen. Twelve-foot tall ceilings create a loft-light space
for the central living and dining area. Open cabinets and shelving creates the illusion of deeper dimensions.

ON THE TOWN

25 Central
Square

Seaside's second major commercial building, 25 Central Square, defines the western border of Seaside's town center and stands as the bookend balancing Dreamland Heights. As prescribed by the Seaside design code, 25 Central Square echoes the scale and mass of Dreamland Heights. In deference to Seaside, architects Rodolfo Machado and Jorge Silvetti favored a spirit of détente between modernism and mainstream Main Street.

From their earliest projects, the Boston firm has boldly conceived and deftly executed urban projects of varying scales and diverse locales. Their designs envision a meaningful architecture of the public realm as well as the particulars of the place. They eschew any single architectural style, but strive to find that which is unique and important within a given project and place, and to express that urbanistically and architecturally.

25 Central Square aspires to the dual demands of a civic and domestic building. Its scale and character are commensurate with the public nature of the important space it addresses. The design revisits the residential/commercial hybrid building, when the concept of "living above the store" was typical of small town business districts. In addition, the architects assimilated elements of Caribbean and Mediterranean vernacular architecture to create an appropriate civic expression specifically suited to Seaside traditions and climate.

(Previous Page)
The four-story building defines the western edge of Seaside's town center.

(Right)
The interiors of the seven apartments coincide with overall form and consistency of external appearance. Large windows and accents of color enliven this living room.

(Opposite)
These two west-facing apartments respect their residential neighbors
with clapboard wood siding and traditional screened porches.

(Above)
The two apartments along the back of the building face the houses of Seaside. Bedrooms located on the fourth floor overlook the one- and two-story cottages.

To create a distinctive profile, the architects surmounted the two stories of commercial space and the double-height colonnade with seven apartments that share a courtyard. The front facade reads like a monumental screen defining the individual apartments with generous roof overhangs and overscaled louvers that work as operable shutters.

The heart of the building is a shared third-floor courtyard that provides access to the seven apartments that occupy the top two floors. Brilliant colors and a dramatic tile pattern create an unexpectedly, vivid space. Punched windows frame selected views to the Gulf.

Each of the five two-story loft-style apartments facing the town center is crowned with its own distinctive pitched roof. Private porches offer each a view the activities of the village and the Gulf of Mexico. Along the backside, the two-story apartments offer a more residential face as they overlook rooftops of the houses of Seaside. Their exteriors are clad in wood and the outdoor rooms are finished as traditional screen porches.

Machado and Silvetti came to Seaside, not with an attitude but with a thoughtful approach to urban design. They drew from a palette of refined, not rarefied, materials, attentive detailing, and an appreciation of Seaside's traditions as they set out to shape an urban drama along the town square. Out-of-town visitors with these kinds of architectural manners are always welcome.

A shared trellised courtyard enlivened with colorful tile and built-in benches separates the two west-facing apartments. The perch offers an engaging view of the houses of Seaside.

urban by the sea

TOP OF THE WORLD

Reddoch
Townhouse

For a house at the beach, there should be few rules. And rules are meant to be broken. The carefree artiste and the unconventional spirit dare to disregard the norms of society and dictates of fashion. Antiques dealer and interior designer Lynn Field Reddoch has a passion for provenance and history. The mood of her third-floor home and ground-floor antique shop is sumptuous theatrical pastiche. A scramble of color and texture and art, the house is decidedly European in approach.

Inside and out, the building is a chronicle of her own sheer nerve and sense of adventure. Lynn bows to the spirit of a continental salon for the single room that occupies the better part of the third floor. She has taken one large space and divided by function it into several smaller areas—space for dining, conversation and cooking.

Hand-painted shutters by artist Lesa Rowe frame the front door. Mounted on operable sliders, the shutters can be opened to take advantage of the view off the verandah or closed for privacy and a colorful background for dining.

To define the kitchen area, Lynn adapted an antique Romanian pine chest to function as working island. The chest was large enough to accommodate a cook top, as well as side drawers for storage and a large butcher block chopping board. Faux finishes by Libby Fillingim enhance the room's old-world charm.

"I try to avoid one dominate style overtaking an entire space," says the designer. "I prefer an eclectic approach that makes my antiques

seem less stiff and formal." Hand-painted panels cleverly hide a television and music system mounted above the fireplace.

"My original scheme provided a day bed in the large living room," recalls Lynn. "While I was moving in, my bed was stored temporarily in the large closet down the hallway. I slept in the dark and cloistered room my first night and decided that would be my permanent bedroom." A cleverly mounted Murphy bed in an antique sideboard allows the small room to function as both a small bedroom and an efficiently arranged space for storage.

Framing the entrance to Ruskin Place, outdoor rooms take on additional responsibilities. Her third-floor verandah serves as a gracious open-air foyer with a wonderful vantage point to monitor the activities of the town.

A painted floor rug enlivens the terrace and offers a most welcoming touch at the front door. A cozy conversation area composed of a wicker love seat and a Gothic-inspired vintage armchair is a precursor of things to come.

The fourth-floor rooftop terrace takes advantage of views of the activities of the amphitheater and the Lyceum, and of course, the Gulf of Mexico. Equally passionate about past styles and artful embellishments for this outdoor room, Lynn positioned barstools along a custom-design table with a wrought-iron base and inlaid tile, at the perfect height to savor a sunset. When entertaining, an antique quilt crafted of beaded fabrics adds a touch of elegance to a simple round table and complements the home's yellow ochre stucco walls and stained concrete floor.

Bold colors and varied textures add welcomed contrasts to the main living area.

(Opposite)
The bathroom functions as both the master bath and the powder room.
An antique stove, adapted by the designer years ago, provides an
interesting focal point. An antique wood panel with leaded glass
panes screens the bathtub.

(Above)
When the Murphy bed recedes into the antique sideboard, this tiny bedroom doubles as a cozy reading nook and the apartment's major storage area.

STAIRWAY TO HEAVEN

Gorlin Townhouse

Architect Alexander Gorlin understands the importance of a grand entrance. This Ruskin Place townhouse attests to that. Designed in the early 1990s for himself, the building consciously exploits the design freedom inherent in an architect's own home.

First and foremost, the 2,200-square-foot house is a celebration of circulation. The process starts with an open-air stairway that appears as a modern interpretation of the open loggias of Italian houses on a piazza or the public stoop of an urban townhouse. Ascending to the second-floor living area, the stairway sets the stage for an unabashedly theatrical structure. Demanding to see and be seen, the house is defined by a double-height glass cube that frames views of the lively urban park, Ruskin Place.

"It's intended to be both the actor and the audience," says Alexander Gorlin. "The expansive wall of glass is the theater's curtain." Following that logic, the living room offers a prime box seat view down to the activities of Ruskin Place. Conversely, the park could be considered the orchestra pit and the floor seats.

The exterior is essentially modernist with its planar surfaces and simplified forms. Ornamentation is strictly structural and functional. A bright red I-beam accentuates the corner while cantilevered balconies define the front and back elevations.

Circulation elements thread through the house, crossing from one side to the other, activating spaces through an ascending procession of architectural elements. Evocative of a ziggurat, each ascending staircase decreases in size and complexity as its rises upward. Moving through the house via the staircase reveals constant delights. The stairs finally emerge on the roof deck, spiraling up to a crow's nest from which to view the Gulf of Mexico.

At night, the townhouse appears as a glowing cube with a solid mass. City rooftops have long invited architectural inspiration. As Seaside's most urban space, Ruskin Place boasts it fair share of architectural eccentricities, including this circular stairway.

A sculptural circular stairway rises thought the tall living room. Floor-to-ceiling windows anchor the dramatic corner view and accentuate the volume of the room's almost square dimensions.

The equally intriguing interiors are a play of solids and voids within the structure's geometric form. Spaces unfold with deliberate ambiguity as edges wrap views from one volume to another. Befitting the architecture's sculptural minimalism, furnishings follow suit. A few choice pieces complement the open plan. A mainstay of modernism, a Corbu chaise longue anchors the front corner. A white leather sofa and kidney-shaped coffee table round out the arrangement.

By the early 1990s, Alexander Gorlin was moving from his early oeuvre of more classically inspired designs to a more consistent modernism. He has designed four other houses along Ruskin Place. Seaside residents Colleen and Sam Yarborough appreciate the breadth and depth of his design virtuosity as much as anyone. The couple first purchased his "Eclipse" townhouse, which presents a decidedly more classically inspired facade to the park while offering a contemporary arrangement of interiors spaces. A few years later, they purchased this townhouse. A repeat homeowner is obviously a happy homeowner.

The dining room is tucked in a cantilevered bay, enlivened with a mix of varied shaped windows. This bay supports the master bedroom's third floor terrace.

(Opposite)
For many Ruskin Place residents, a large appeal of Seaside is the view.
Directly across the park is another townhouse designed by Alexander Gorlin.

(Above)
The master bedroom is located along the back of the third floor and opens onto a more private terrace facing west.
Color is limited to a large French bistro poster above the bed, a single chair, and the door. The narrow stairway leads to the roof terrace.

CULTIVATED VIEW

coastal classic

Renfroe House

(Previous Page)
The site's irregular configuration, roughly the shape of a horseshoe, allows the large building to be broken into a series of pavilions anchored by the commanding tower.

(Right)
The second-floor living room is outfitted in an inviting taupe-and-cream palette. The ceiling's peak roof, the limestone fireplace, and textures bring added dimensions to the neutral tones. The tortoise shell now occupies a prominent spot above the fireplace.

(Below)
In this vacation atmosphere, life revolves around the outdoor spaces. This generous veranda, with its overhangs and series of ceiling fans, ensures the space is comfortable in any weather.

Let it not be for present delight, nor for present use alone; let it be such work as our descendants will thank us for.

—*John Ruskin*

Self-avowed "beach people," Patty and Charlie Renfroe found a lot to like about the town of Seaside and its glorious stretch of sand and surf. When one of Seaside's largest home sites on Smolian Circle became available, they knew this was the perfect place for a second home.

The Atlanta couple turned to local architect Thomas Christ to design a gathering spot large enough to lure their four children, spouses, and eight grandchildren for vacations and holidays at the beach.

The house reflects a grace and elegance in its architectural aspirations. Subtle allusions to the Shingle Style, with its expansive forms and gracious proportions, give the house its distinctive character. With its commanding tower, reminiscent of favorite fairy tale, the Renfroe home seems to transcend time. Yet, there is nothing imposing or pretentious about the house, thanks to its gentle placement on the site and the deft handling of traditional details and materials.

The charm of the house begins with the enticing pathway to the sheltered front breezeway. Landscape designer Randy Harelson enhanced the site's lush native landscape by draping Confederate jassamine over picket fences and planting magnolias and live oaks, judiciously, to balance the scale of the tower.

Thomas Christ and interior designer Toby West worked together to ensure this new house would have the patina and timeworn appeal of an older home while providing rooms and functions befitting a contemporary lifestyle. To accommodate the large extended family and afford privacy for all, the house is organized into distinct zones. The master suite is positioned on the second floor.

Guest bedrooms and a bunkroom for the grandchildren open off a family room on the first floor with easy connection to the screened porch and private swimming pool. A separate apartment, accessed through the tower, can be closed off for rental or opened up for large family gatherings.

Equally as sophisticated as the floor plan is the interior décor. A palette of sandy tones and nautical themes permeate throughout. The concept started with an antique tortoise shell from the Toby West's antique shop. The coastal theme continued with an impressive collection of pond yachts mounted along the stairway and positioned in other prominent spots around the house. Baskets of seashells, navigational maps, and prints of shorebirds and shells repeat the motif.

One of the joys of the beach is spending time out of doors in every sort of weather. The house has deep covered verandahs on both the first and second floor, a side porch, back screened porch, and crow's nest in the tower.

The strength of this house is a breath of comfort and sophistication. This isn't a house that overwhelms or overpowers. It is a house with a livable harmony, which allows first-time visitors and old family friends to move about the rooms with the same sense of belonging as children and grandchildren.

Inside and out, the home appears as if it was poured from a single pitcher with architect, interior designer, and builder working together with a shared goal to conjure up a building that merges effortlessly with its setting and the seasons.

Clearly, they have created the setting for a lifetime of unforgettable adventures and cherished days and nights. "This place has become such an important part of all us," says Patty. "It's such a wonderful retreat from the rest of the world." Their Seaside home also promises to be a legacy for descendants to appreciate thankfully for years to come.

(Previous Page)
*French doors open onto the second-floor veranda connecting
indoor and outdoor dining areas. Old and new mingles effortlessly. An antique
clock stands along the wall; the chandelier is a custom design by Toby West.*

(Above)
*The engaging blend of varied influences continues into the grandchildren's bunk room. Starfish are mounted on the walls against patterned wallpaper.
Storage is in a nineteenth-century antique chest and pull-drawers mounted under the bunks.*

(Opposite)
Mellow tones and delicate fabrics permeate the master suite. An antique writing desk occupies one wall; built-in wall units offer practical storage.

BUILT FOR KEEPS

coastal classic

Hudson House

From the beginning, people were drawn to Seaside because it was a real community, a place to be filled with real houses, not anonymous resort addresses. From the first time Suellen Hudson visited the fledgling coastal village in the early 1980s, she "got it" immediately. Her husband Hal needed a little more convincing.

Somewhat reluctantly, he agreed to purchase a home site under the condition that Suellen would oversee every aspect of designing and building a vacation house. With a simple set of plans drawn up by architect Carey McWhorter, she assembled carpenters and subcontractors and built a classic Florida cracker cottage on Savannah Street.

Just when the Hudsons were ready to move in, they got one of those offers you can't refuse from a couple who wanted to buy a completed house, not property. To sweeten the deal Robert Davis offered Suellen and Hal another lot, and Suellen set out to build her second home. Suellen built five more bungalows (see Helvie Cottage on page 36) before she decided it was time to give up the temporary address for a permanent vacation home.

Seaside's architectural codes called for various types of structures depending on the street and neighborhood. Their earlier houses had been modest designs, but the prominent lot on Seaside Avenue called for a more ambitious house with continuous double porches and columns. One recommended prototype for the street was the Greek Revival mansion of the Antebellum South.

Suellen and Hal set out on an exhaustive research of appropriate models, which led them to Waverly Plantation, a classic 1852 Greek Revival home in Columbus, Mississippi. They turned to Tampa architect Don Cooper, who had designed several houses in Seaside including his own family vacation retreat.

With an intuitive understanding of the past-in-the-present quality, Don melded old and new to emulate a historic landmark while designing an utterly livable house for the beach. "I had drawn a basic floor plan and

(Previous Page)
The home's artful composition and two-story columns make
for a confident demeanor. Wide porches on both floors are the
perfect spot for entertaining or simply rocking quietly.

(Above)
Innovation can be inspiring, but often an understated room can be so engaging it doesn't seem to matter if it's conventional or cutting edge.
A pair of matching love seats centered along the fireplace creates an intimate conversation area within the larger space.

elevations," recalls Suellen. "Don showed me that a talented architect's understanding of scale and proportion brings so much to the process."

The classic four-square house was completed in 1992, and today stands comfortably ensconced amid sheltering oaks. Like its historical antecedent, this house reflects a penchant for symmetry, balance, and tried-and-true classical forms.

The first glimpse of the house with its picket fence, welcoming double front porches, and ornate railings evokes a happy homecoming, while the two-story pillars and octagonal cupola impart a grandeur befitting the house's setting and station.

Once inside, the traditional four-square plan gives way to a more contemporary cadence of interconnected spaces. "A house should have large rooms and cozy little spaces to foster a variety of uses and experiences," says Don Cooper. A series of columns rather than a solid wall allows the living room to take advantage of the fourteen-foot-wide center hall. As a counterpoint to the gracious living room, a small reading nook anchors a sunny corner along the back of the house.

An ethos of neutrals and moderation sets the tone for the interior décor. "For the earlier houses, we had taken a more casual approach and used a lot of color," recalls Suellen. "I was ready for more textures and a neutral palette of sandy tones." Working with interior designer Chip McAlpine, Suellen balances the formal arrangement and traditional details of the architecture with casually elegant furniture and a mix of antiques.

On the second floor, four equally sized bedrooms anchor the home's four corners. Decorated with a warm palette of colors, each bedroom has its own personality and presence.

(Right)
A mix of neutral fabrics and simple antique furniture create restful, comfortable spaces in both the living room and the cozy reading nook.

(Opposite)
The unifying element is a grand stairway,
a work of art in itself rising up through the
house to the third-floor observation tower.

(Above)
Late afternoon sunlight dances through the dining room. Antiques are arranged in a more contemporary manner to encourage a sense of flow between rooms.

coastal classic

ON THE AVENUE

Flores
House

(Previous Page)
The house commands respect without shouting for attention, thanks to double porches running the full width of the house and a discreet rooftop tower.

(Above)
A collection of timeless teak furniture enlivens the deep front porch.

First impressions can be lasting impressions. That's certainly true of this classically inspired house designed by Thomas Christ. The congenial front porch and attention to detail offer a telling introduction to the style and personality that radiates throughout the home of Cherie and Jim Flores.

The Floreses are an active family. With four young children, a place at the beach demands to be a lived-in house. But they also wanted a gracious retreat befitting its prominent location on Seaside Avenue. The house proudly embodies classical and vernacular traditions, while the planning is very open with light and airy interiors and all the perfunctory conveniences families require today. There's an implied formality in the architecture and detailing, while rooms are defined by subtle references and traditional framed openings rather than solid walls.

For all its bows to tradition, the house has more than its share of contemporary touches. To ensure a decorating style compatible with the architecture, Cherie worked closely with interior designer Jamie Christ. The owner's impressive collection of art glass set the tone for the décor and establishes an inspiring color palette. Bold strokes of blue and green are perfect tones for a house along a stretch of beach called the Emerald Coast.

The generous living room calls out for large-scale art and furnishings. A large painting rests above the overstuffed sofa upholstered in soft blue denim. The dining room mingles the familiar and the unexpected. A contemporary dining table, accented with bands of silver, pairs with eight chairs with tall narrow backs of woven jute.

(Right)
Touches like a stainless steel display cabinet in a corner of the dining room introduce an element of surprise.

Throughout the house, tall double-hung windows are used in abundance to ensure plenty of natural light. Window treatments are simple and flowing. Their height adds drama, but in a casual way.

The house also reflects the architect's talent for creating spaces with multiple personalities. More than ceremonial space, a grand stair hall doubles as a comfortable family room. The television and stereo system are tucked under the staircase, opposite a curving built-in sofa with plump cushions and an abundance of colorful throw pillows. The high placement of the large window offers privacy and still allows for an interesting play of light, while the double-height ceiling adds to the bright and welcoming feel of the space.

In a commitment to conviviality, the house has a large live-in kitchen structured for entertaining and outdoor dining. The kitchen's side door opens to a screened porch secluded by louvered shutters along the street wall.

The floor plan also allows for public and private spaces to be just that. Pocket doors permit the downstairs hallway to be closed off from the kitchen and family room, affording the master suite an added layer of privacy. The mood changes in the master suite. Light finishes give way to dark woods and luxurious fabrics in deep colors, reflecting a preference for a compatible contradiction. A built-in seat with book shelves on either end is tucked in the bay window. The children's bedrooms are all located upstairs.

For all its classical leanings, the house has a great flow and wonderful sense of openness. The tripartite window set high above the built-in sofa creates a dramatic setting for the stairway and family room.

Bold splashes of blue and green are the unifying theme throughout the living spaces. Although an implied formality is established with identical armoires flanking the fireplace, a casual arrangement of overstuffed sofas and comfortable chairs immediately relaxes the space.

(Opposite)
Butterflies and botanical prints are the inspiration
for this upstairs bedroom. Soothing greens and
flowing linens create a restful retreat.

(Above)
The mood of the master suite is a deliberate departure of the living spaces. The cool blues and greens,
give way to a palette of sand and earth tones, dark woods, and textured linens and silks.

beach contemporary

POETIC LICENSE

Reinhard
House

Leaving though wanting to stay,
Needing to "get back to it"
What's it?
The challenge to take peace and stillness,
Find vistas of sand, water, trees, thoughtfully built forms.
(Elements of childlikeness?)
Back to it?
To delight in the soft breeze, the face, the hand, the light.
How brief our time here,
How fragile each heart.

Architect Aldo Rossi wrote these words on a visit to Seaside during the schematic design of a home for Sarah and Don Reinhard. He left the poem in the guest journal of his rental cottage. "We happened to spend the night in the same cottage as we were moving into the house and found the poem," says Sarah.

While other architects might have been struggling with programs and budgets, Aldo Rossi was focused on more ethereal issues of design and life. The poignant words later took on deeper meaning. The architect passed away in a tragic automobile accident soon after the house was completed.

The house is a befitting work of remembrance for the architect and stands as an important introduction to Seaside. Most visitors approach the town from the west, so this house is the first they see. In spirit and stance, the house immediately evokes countless beloved images of the South with an equal measure of humility and grandeur and all the while possessing a lighthearted and contemporary character all its own.

A pretty tall order for a house. For just these reasons, Seaside designated five prominent architects for the site. Sarah and Don purchased the property with the condition they would hire one of the five from the list. "We had never built a house from scratch," recalls Sarah. "And we certainly had never worked with a world-famous architect." After research and interviews, the Reinhards selected Italian architect Aldo Rossi and his New York City-based partner Morris Adjmi. "From our first meetings as we walked around Seaside, it was clear they understood what we wanted in our home," says Don.

(Previous Page)
This engaging waterfront house more than fulfills the promised implied by its entrance. Identical vaulted carports dominate the front façade and announce the home's symmetry that continues throughout.

(Opposite)
An addition was built five years after the original house was completed. The two-story wing bridges the sandy footpath to create a ground-floor screen porch amid the landscape.

(Below)
A tall window anchors a cozy corner of the new sunroom. The sunroom extends out and over the footpath.

The interiors were never intended to overwhelm or overpower. The new sunroom exudes a relaxed elegance and boasts a masterful play of natural light. Overstuffed upholstered chairs are as comfortable as a favorite swimsuit cover-up and a seagrass rug camouflages the inevitable tracks of sand.

*The original living and dining room possess a gracious openness. Interior furnishings are
deliberately subtle so nothing takes away from the view. Colors are muted earth tones.*

The Reinhards charged the architects to create a house at once distinctive while conforming to the character of the town. "Aldo was also interested in our needs and desires," says Don. "Here was a very famous architect, and he really listened to us."

This house, like the architect's other structures, eschews literal precedents in favor of a reinterpretation of familiar forms and recognizable icons. "We set out to strike a balance between a home in keeping with the spirit of Seaside and a landmark building that stood out.

Classical forms sets up visual expectations, and the architects' use of symmetry and stripped down classical elements exploits the tension between the landscape, the axial arrangement of rooms, and the house itself.

The strength of the house lies is in its erudite arrangement of everyday shapes and symbols to create a memorable image. The monumental exterior is a testament to the architect's preference for simple materials and forms. A pair of Doric columns and overscaled pilaster supporting the front corner of the roof deck creates a grand entrance. Along the beachside, the formality loosens up where a wing extends out and over the footpath.

Equally engaging as the romantic entrance is the wonderful atmosphere inside, which unfolds as one reaches the top of the stair to find an unsurpassed view of the Gulf. The arrangement of rooms mimics the exterior's symmetry, as well as its precise proportions, and subtle architectural detailing.

Inside and out, this home is animated with forms that have been transformed. It is a home that is original without being novel, playful without being coy, refreshingly simple in appearance but complex in content.

If a home is choreography of architecture, its inhabitants are the dancers. Don and Sarah Reinhard play their roles well on a refined and complex stage that is gracious, inviting, and totally appropriate for its glorious setting.

(Opposite) A mix of light and dark woods and stainless enliven the galley kitchen defined by a counter with seating.

In the kitchen, a whimsical tile pattern designed by the architect recalls cabanas lined up along the beach.

STRUCTURAL SAVOIR-FAIRE

Appell Cottage

There's no question that this is a beach house. But it's not a conventional cottage by the sea. Proud yet playful, Roger and Diane Appell's Seaside home, designed by architect Victoria Casasco, is a building with a bit of an attitude.

Seaside's town architect in 1987, Victoria remembers how she was intrigued by the traditional building process. "I loved watching houses as they were going up on Tupelo Street," she says. "They seemed much more interesting when you could see the raw bones of the wood-frame structure exposed."

Among the earliest published photographs of Seaside, the quintessential images were of Rosewalk's Victorian cottages rendered in pastel hues and animated with fanciful detailing. Many potential clients were drawn to these more romantic expressions and didn't necessarily share Victoria's aesthetics. Roger Appell was open to exploring more contemporary interpretations of the familiar residential forms.

Appropriately called Roger's Lighthouse, the building delights in the manipulation of light and composition through the creation of a labyrinth of structure, walls, and windows. An elegant abstraction of Southern vernacular wood-frame construction, the 2,400-square-foot house proudly exposes the adorned bracing of its structural skeleton and reveals its wood cladding as the exterior skin.

This bold structural display assures the building is firmly anchored to the landscape, yet the house remains open, engaging and transparent. This transparency between the interior and exterior establishes a complex spatial relationship. Indoor rooms live like the outdoors; outdoor spaces live like indoor rooms. "Nine months of the year, the temperate climate of Northwest Florida is conducive to living in an open-air environment," maintains the architect. "Every space in the house is designed to take advantage of the setting and the seasons."

Turned inside out, the bones of the traditional wood-frame construction carve out a deep recessed front porch, which extends from

(Previous Page)
A steeply pitched gable roof and an exposed wooden
structure make a memorable first impression.

(Above)
The living room's high ceilings enhance natural ventilation. Double doors open onto the deep front porch.
A few large pieces of furniture upholstered in simple white cotton are in keeping with the scale of the room.

the living area and embraces the street while maintaining a subtle gradation of privacy between the public and private sectors.

The home's unique layering of forms and structures also supports an encircling verandah with a shuttered living room on the second floor. Inspired by Caribbean sleeping porches, this gracious open-air space is wrapped on all four sides with floor-to-ceiling wooden louvers that swing open to panoramic views of the rooftops of the town and Gulf beyond, as well as capture the breezes from every direction. The steeply pitched metal roof, exposed trusses, and whirling ceiling fans make for outdoor living rooms that are comfortable day and night throughout most of the year. "There's no better place to sit out a summer storm with the sound of rain drops rapping on the tin roof," says the owner.

The home's interior spaces, though refined, are restrained in comparison to the dramatic exterior. Walls and ceilings are lightly whitewashed plywood patterned with a grid of board-and-batten. Rather than solid walls, partitions of solids and voids reminiscent of a Piet Mondrian painting define simple volumes and encourage interplay between relatively small rooms on the first floor. Narrow stairways and a series of small mezzanines and balconies make for a most intriguing arrangement of spaces on the upper floors while affording the individual bedrooms privacy and separation.

The elevated stature of this fairly small house comes from the ingenious and intricate way it defines space and structure, creating a home that is utterly livable and aesthetically engaging.

(Right)
Although color is used sparingly inside, an accent wall of orange marks the stairway. The layering of voids and solids allows rooms to unfold, creating long views through the house.

*The back of the house is animated with varying plays on
scale and proportions including vertical windows and doors,
an asymmetrical second-floor balcony, and a rooftop sundeck.*

*A space that's half-in, half-out, the second-floor shutter room possesses a magical interchange with nature. Furniture is a mix of antique wicker and rattan
with accent colors and vintage fabrics that nod to old Florida. A towering palm set in a built-in planter anchors a corner of the room.*

beach contemporary

SEEING RED

Dahlgren House

The adage "don't judge a book by its cover" has always applied beyond literary works. Ann Houston Dahlgren's home certainly deserves a thorough investigation before reaching a design verdict. From a distance, the house strikes a dramatic silhouette against a bright blue sky. And its succulent shade of red has no equal in town. Not only is it a bold departure from the approved palette, no color evokes more emotions than red—danger, embarrassment, love, hate, and passion.

Architect Charles Warren, who was Seaside's town architect at the time of the design, relishes such ambiguous messages. "Nothing is more modern than classical architecture," he maintains. All detailing, both inside and out, is classically derived with an ordered system of sequence, yet there is nothing overly ornate.

The house is a tapestry of themes as diverse as villas dating from antiquity to the Panhandle's long-standing traditions of wood-frame construction. Charles acknowledges the Roman villa of Pliny the Younger as inspiration. "My goal was a house that gently mediates between man and nature," says Charles. "It is arranged around specific orientations to the sun, the sea, and the winds."

The approach to and the movement through the house are orchestrated to disclose its secrets gradually. A simple cloistered portico offers the first impression. Inward and upward from this simple cubic entryway, the house unfolds as a series of explicitly classical episodes.

(Previous Page)
An ensemble of bold forms and a dramatic shade of red give this home its distinctive stance. Lush native vegetation envelopes the house. The rooftop pavilion dominates the composition.

(Right)
Each of the loggias and porches is treated differently. The second-floor's more public veranda takes full advantage of the gable roofline, exposed trusses, and a lively combination of golden yellows and blue trim.

This sequence is articulated with increasingly specific classical ornamentation. A long gentle stair spirals around the exterior of the house offering views along the way of the town center of Seaside. The ascent culminates in a tower pavilion as apex. Animated with Tuscan columns, the pavilion is the home's indisputable signature. Affording views in every direction, it looks out westward across a park and the setting sun and southward to the Odessa Street Pavilion and Gulf of Mexico.

Interiors possess a refreshing openness and sense of light. The rooms' proportions echo the ratios of the golden section. Living spaces are on the second level, above the ground floor bedrooms, to create a *piano nobile*. This configuration assures a degree of privacy in the densely built town.

The colors and furnishing take a decided turn towards creams and neutrals, offering a cool respite from the intensity of the climate. Much of the architectural ornament stems from the building's construction, including exposed beams, rafters, and purlins of the ceilings. Decorative objects interpret the themes of the architecture including a lantern on the stairway pillar and emphasize more fanciful elements of living at the beach.

Inside and outside, classical or contemporary, this is definitely a house to escape to with friends and extended family. "Our families have been coming to Seaside for spring break for years," says Ann's sister-in-law Krista Russell. "We love everything about Seaside—the town, the beach, and of course, Ann's red house."

(Right)
Tuscan columns march along the tower pavilion to frame views of the town. The pavilion and an adjoining open air deck offer a variety of outdoor experiences. One is cloistered within the sheltering arms of the columns; the other is completely open to the sun.

(Opposite)
Every room, both indoors and out, establish a sequence of relating proportions. A replica of the home's pavilion serves as a lantern set atop a pillar at the top of the stairway landing. A central island offers casual dining in the sunny kitchen.

In the master bathroom, tumbled marble tile and a pair of pedestal sinks infuse a refinement of finishes without a hint of opulence.

(Above)
Architectural features, including square pillars, offer a subtle demarcation between the living room and dining room.

beach contemporary

OF THE DUNES

Childs / Zaret
House

(Previous Page)
The house nestles behind the dune line amid lush vegetation.
Garden designer Randy Harelson enhanced the settings with
native plantings hearty enough to withstand the elements.

(Opposite)
An arch frames the front door and sets
the stage for streamlined spaces inside.

(Above)
A pair of French doors offers a welcoming interchange between the master suite and the screen sleeping porch. Textured silks and bed linens harmonize with subtle colors of natural woods and nature. A coral Utrecht chair designed by Gerrit Rietveld in the 1930s anchors the corner.

Florida was never on their list of places to live. Joan Childs and Jerry Zaret were quite content in New York City. In the late 1980s, however, the urban couple was intrigued by several articles in national design and travel magazines touting the virtues of Seaside ("a new town, the old ways") along the Gulf of Mexico. "I didn't believe there were beaches anywhere in Florida—or the continental United States for that matter—that were as beautiful as the photographs," recalls Joan. "We decided to see for ourselves."

From their first visit, the aquamarine waters, the sugar white sand, and the architecture of the town exceeded their expectations. One trip led to another, and it wasn't long before the couple had purchased a prime gulf-front property. By 1995 construction commenced on a 2,350-square-foot house designed by architects Richard Gibbs and Ty Nunn, which now serves as their primary residence during the spring and fall.

Design codes, mandating a low, lean profile to protect views of the beach and to respect the dramatic setting, prompted the architects to look to the principles and prairie-style houses of Frank Lloyd Wright for inspiration. Responding to Wright's dictum that "no house should ever be on a hill or on anything. It should be of the hill," the two-story structure nestles within the lush vegetation of scrub oak and magnolias behind the primary dune line.

Rather than a literal interpretation of Prairie style, Wright's influence resonates in details, materials and forms. Strong horizontal lines, dramatic arches, deep-set windows, and massive white floating columns dominate the form of the house. A respect for the nature of materials is expressed on the exterior with an animated pattern of lead-coated copper work while horizontal board-and-batten wood siding anchors the structure to the land.

A low archway boldly marks the front door. This embracing first impression gives way to a spacious double-height foyer crowned with a barrel ceiling, which is accentuated with

curving wooden strips and a *shoji* screen backlit for a diffused glow. Four massive pillars frame the floating stairway that rises through the heart of the house.

The high ceiling, combined with the play of natural light, opens up the house and entices visitors upstairs where splendor of the interiors unfold. The living and dining areas and kitchen are not a formal chambering of events but a more contemporary response with open spaces flowing one to another. Floor-to-ceiling windows accentuated with a gentle arch frame views to the east and west, while a bank of three oversized French doors opens onto the large second-floor porch. Window treatments are nonexistent upstairs.

Both upstairs and downstairs, rooms wrapped in gleaming maple accentuated and accented with mahogany trim create a warm canvas for Joan and Jerry's eclectic collection of furniture, art, and accessories. Like Wright who worked with his clients on designing details of the interiors, Richard helped select colors and furnishings to echo the sophisticated understated architecture of the house. Curvilinear tables, and low-slung sofas and chairs upholstered in subtle shades of cool citrons and warm melons complement the clean lines of the interior architecture. A custom dining room table designed by the architect is crafted of black ash with a long elliptical form evocative of an oversized surfboard.

Each of the two bedrooms features a built-in platform bed, wall-mounted side tables, and storage units to reinforce the horizontal wood banding. Subtle details and elegant materials define the functions of rooms and instill the house with a sense of inevitability and intimacy. Inside and out, scale and volume engender distinct and lasting impressions regardless of the vantage point from which the house is experienced.

(Opposite)
*The house capitalizes on the relationship between inside and out.
A thicket of scrub oak envelops the downstairs screen porch.
Cotton draperies fluttering in the wind and a pair of swinging
daybeds make for an inviting sleeping porch both day and night.*

(Above)
*The expressive qualities of the mahogany and maple are explored in structure and ornamental detailing. Natural sunlight
becomes an added finish as it rakes across surfaces and textures, bringing them to life throughout the day.*

(Opposite Page)
The curves of the dining room table and chairs complement
the geometry of the raised paneling, exposed beams, and
columns. Handrails are finely honed, as one might find on
a handmade Shaker object, while metal hardware details
add contemporary elegance.

(Above)
Substantial floating columns frame the views of the Gulf. Chaise lounges and small tables are
deliberately low to echo the horizontal lines of the interiors without infringing on the vista.

OPEN TO DISCUSSION

Chatham
Dog Trot

(Previous Page)
Florida's earliest beach houses were often wood frame, raised off the ground for better circulation and to avoid rising water, primarily shuttered, and roofed in tin. This house acknowledges those precedents while proclaiming allegiance to the present.

(Opposite)
Starting with the front door, there's a kind of a prosaic Southern charm in the unpretentious look of this cluster of forms that make up this house.

(Above)
With all the panel doors closed, the house assumes a playful checker-board appearance.

For anyone who thought Seaside was only lollipop pastels, gingerbread trim, and picturesque picket fences, architect Walton Chatham proved them wrong in 1987 with the completion of this home for his wife and two young children.

The house was affectionately and unofficially dubbed the "dog trot" for its abstracted references to the nineteenth-century— and far from glamorous—architectural antecedent. A dogtrot is a rural dwelling, according to Southern folklore, where a shaded breezeway offered respite for a hound on a hot summer day when animals lived outdoors and no one had air conditioning.

Inspired by simple geometry and the potential of mundane material, Walter joyfully reinterpreted familiar forms in a fresh and highly personal idiom. He refuted the conventional wisdom that a house must imitate tradition to be regional and shun historical references to be contemporary. In doing so, he proved just how flexible Seaside's ostensibly strict design codes could be.

Although the house was, and still is, decidedly different from its neighbors, it's really an old-fashioned, common-sense way of building that responds to the climate and available materials. Inspired by old tobacco barns and boat sheds, Walter divided the 1,800-square-foot house into two separate wings that sit atop a raised wooden plinth.

Each of the two pavilions is constructed of a strapping unpainted wood frame with three-by-ten-inch pine posts and nine-inch beams bolted together and crowned with a steeply pitched metal roof with deep overhangs. In place of conventional walls, the architect designed infill panels in a variety of materials including galvanized steel and glass block for the bathroom. The bold forms and muscular materials denounce once and forever any suggestion of overly romantic historical pretense.

Facing the shared open deck, a series of ten-foot-tall pivotal doors, animated with a checkerboard pattern, are the home's defining feature. Painted black and white on the exterior, the doors swing open to announce a colorful interior rainbow of yellow, coral and blue.

Bedrooms are deliberately sparse. Two single beds with crisp white linens and a single night table are the only furnishings.

The interiors and exteriors are deliberately ambiguous with edges wrapping views from one space to another and out to the center porch. The bedroom wing is set two feet above the shared open deck. The colorful ten-foot panel doors are a defining feature of the house. Thanks to the deep overhangs and angle of the pivoted doors, the interior spaces are protected from direct sunlight most of the day.

Furnishings and decorations throughout the house are spare, ad hoc, and deliberately low-key, to let the architecture speak for itself. A pair of matching cubist club chairs designed by Mary Chatham and two butterfly chairs anchor and define the conversation area. Likewise, the bedrooms are deliberately uncluttered.

The house is a hymnal of living with nature instead of fighting it. Accordingly, finishes and furnishing were chosen to acquiesce to the elements—hot temperature, salt air, moisture, and wind. Marine-grade plywood and paint were used for the panel doors.

The house functions best with all the doors open, obliterating the distinction between indoors and outdoor living. "I grew up in the South," says Walter. "And I believe sultry summer nights are to be savored. The crickets calling out in the darkness, the stars shining above, and condensation dripping off a glass of anything really ice cold."

(Left)
A galvanized barrel vaulted ceiling, rising fifteen feet, crowns the living room. The cubist club chairs were designed by Mary Chatham.

(Opposite)
The two bedrooms share a soaking tub and shower, enlivened by a wall of glass block.

166

beach contemporary

RAISED EXPECTATIONS

Hansbrough House

(Previous Page)   A house in this setting has no backside. One front reaches out to the majesty of the beach while the other front beckons visitors to venture indoors.

(Right)   Nestled amid the native landscape of the dunes, the screen porch opens off the master bedroom and enjoys varying moods as sun and shadows change throughout the day.

There's a demanding duality of a house directly on the water. It must address the best and worst Mother Nature has to offer—one day embracing the splendor of the sun setting into the Gulf and the next day enduring the brunt of a tropical storm. Melanie and Tommy Hansbrough's Seaside home happily responds to the dictates of its glorious setting.

The design and construction of this house is a true collaborative effort. "First, there was Robert's vision and the inspired town plan," maintains Melanie. "Our architect, Alexander Gorlin, is a genius. But our builder, Benoit Laurent is one of the unsung heroes of Seaside. You can't build a town without a master builder. Benoit is a true is artist." And you also need enlightened clients like Melanie and Tommy Hansbrough.

Seaside's covenants dictate long narrow houses on the water. This structure adheres to town rules with a low-pitched, standing-seam metal roof, clapboard siding of Southern pine, and wide overhanging eaves. Although Alexander alludes to indigenous forms, he goes about creating his own concurrent order and in the process augments the elemental power of the natural setting.

The second-floor terrace offers a fresh take on a familiar form with its abstracted pergola. The wooden canopy follows the form and low pitch of the house's metal roof and ever so gracefully filters the harsh Florida sun. Large exterior windows are arranged in a rational grid inspired by Japanese screens.

Inside, the house gradually opens up to its surroundings. The first introduction is the unpretentious foyer. The drama of the interiors unfolds with a staircase bathed in natural light and detailed with maple that ascends to the open and loftlike second floor. This great room is the true heart of the house and readily fulfills the promise of its name. The interconnected living dining kitchen areas are equally conducive to family intimacy as well as holiday gatherings and large parties.

Balancing sleekness and carefully crafted details, the room boasts limestone floors, maple-paneled walls and built-ins, and granite accents in the kitchen. A careful manipulation of interior volumes enhances the feeling of spaciousness.

A series of sturdy pillars, combined with the gently sloping ceiling framed with precise maple trim, instills a broad tentlike volume in the living room—deceptively simple and sublimely ordered.

Two sets of French doors open to the rear porch with unspoiled views of the dunes, the white sandy beach and Gulf of Mexico. A spiral stair descends into a screened-in porch, a room that is simultaneously inside and outside.

Painters have long found inspiration in the ever-changing vistas of the sand and sea. And Melanie is no exception. Views from the house are reflected in the art throughout the house. The screen porch serves as her studio. "It's protected, it's quiet, and it's beautiful," she adds. "My color palette changed remarkably when I started painting in the house. My colors are drawn from these natural surroundings and are much more subdued." The paired paintings over the dining room sideboard are of the stand of pines along Western Lake. Above the fireplace is the third view from a series.

Ironically, it was Melanie who was reluctant to undertake the ambitious process of designing and building this house. She was content with their cottage on West Ruskin Street. It was Tommy who wanted a home directly on the water.

However, some things are just meant to be. "Years before we had even heard of Seaside, I had torn out and saved a photograph from a magazine of my dream house on the beach," recalls Melanie. Years later, when the time came to select an architect for their Gulf-front property, the Hansbroughs started with Seaside's approved list of twelve designers. "The first portfolio we opened at the sales office was Alexander Gorlin's and there was the same photograph of my dream house," says Melanie. It was the beginning of a beautiful friendship.

A wood frame pergola animates the second floor porch, multiplying the shadow lines while retaining views upwards. "We love the open design," says Melanie. "At night we can sit on the deck and look up to see the stars." A circular stairway descends to the more protected ground-floor screen porch.

174

ACKNOWLEDGMENTS

We are grateful for the generosity, kindness, and support of all who assisted with this book. Our deepest thanks go to Daryl and Robert Davis, whose vision led to the creation of this remarkable and influential town along the Gulf of Mexico. Without their encouragement and support, this project would not have been possible.

Our deepest thanks go to the homeowners who embraced the vision of Seaside and infused the town with their own striking individuality. They graciously opened their homes to us—and to our readers. We also acknowledge the artistic vision and technical skills of the architects, designers, and builders whose houses are featured.

We are indebted to Stacey May Brady, Seaside's Director of Public Relations and Marketing, for her patience, professionalism, and humor. Her assistance with the photography and the historical research was indispensable. Jacqueline Joyce Barker, James Pinckard, and Donna Marie Spiers were most helpful with the selection process—sometimes literally opening the doors of the houses of Seaside. We thank Erica Pierce and Susan Byrd of Pizitz Home & Cottage for providing furnishings and accessories that help define Seaside Style. We also thank Andrea Oppenheimer Dean and Nellie DeBruyn for proofreading the text and offering architectural insights.

A few others require special thanks. We express our gratitude to the individuals who make Seaside a genuine community. We are particularly grateful to the Modica family, whose Old World grocery was our source for great coffee and welcome smiles in the morning. Linda and Bob White of Sundog Books are tireless supporters of authors who promote not just the story of Seaside, but of important architecture and design in general. We also thank Dave Rauschkolb and Scott Witcoski for creating Bud & Alley's, the perfect place to unwind after a long day.

For their encouragement and hospitality, we thank Dorothy Baratta, Cliff Holtermann, Carolyn and Rusty Goldsmith, Diane Helvie, Mary Moore Hoover, Craige Hoover, Leah and Willie Mason, Lourdes Reynafarje, and Sheree Williams.

Our sincerest thanks go to David Morton for his support of this project and his editorial guidance and to the staff of Rizzoli for their assistance in the production of the book.

—*Steven Brooke & Eleanor Lynn Nesmith*